CHRONICLE BOOKS

SAN FRANCISCO

First published in the United States in 2003 by Chronicle Books LLC

Introduction and texts copyright © 2003 by Mel Gooding

Alphabet from *Species of Spaces and Other Pieces* by Georges Perec, translated by John Sturrock (Penguin, 1997) copyright © 1997 by John Sturrock

Pages 216–221 constitute a continuation of the copyright page.

Library of Congress Cataloging-in-Publication Data available.

ISBN 0-8118-3981-8

Manufactured in Hong Kong

Cover design: Azi Rad

Distributed in Canada by Raincoast Books
9050 Shaughnessy Street
Vancouver, British Columbia V6P 6E5

10 9 8 7 6 5 4 3 2 1

Chronicle Books LLC
85 Second Street
San Francisco, California 94105

www.chroniclebooks.com

Research and design: Julian Rothenstein
Texts: Mel Gooding
Consultant: Lutz Becker
Artwork: Terence Smiyan, Marit Münzberg
Production: Tim Chester

Grateful acknowledgment is made to the following:

Merrill C. Berman, Jim Frank
The Merrill C. Berman Collection, New York

PhDr Iva Janáková, PhDr Koenigsmarkova, Alena Zapletalová
The Museum of Decorative Arts, Prague

Kerstin Hinkel, Norbert Kaut
The Gutenberg-Museum, Mainz

Dr. Stefan Soltek, Martina Weisz
The Klingspoor Museum, Offenbach

Bertram Schmidt-Friderichs, Brigitte Raab
Verlag Hermann Schmidt, Mainz

Nigel Roache, Denise Roughan
St Bride's Printing Library, London

Pauline Rae, Jeremy Aynsley
The Royal College of Art, London

Martin Andrews
Department of Typography and Graphic Communication at The University of Reading, Middlesex

David Batterham
David Batterham Rare Books, London

Xavier Bermúdez
Trama Visual, Mexico City

David Hillman, Sally Waterman
Pentagram, London

Wolfgang Hartmann
Fundación Tipografía Bauer, Barcelona

Walter R. Wybrands
BV Uitgeverij D Bataafsche Leeuw/Van Soeren & Co, Amsterdam

Neil Handley
British Optical Association Museum/The College of Optometrists, London

Michael Collinge, Oliver Clark
Collinge & Clark, London

Jan Tholenaar
The Jan Tholenaar Collection, Amsterdam

Brian Webb
Trickett & Webb, London

Thanks also to: Hiang Kee, Richard Hollis, Alan Fletcher, David Wakefield, Jan Solpera, Misha Anikst, Alan E. Rapp, Janet Pilch, Marcela Ramirez, Piers Wardle, John L.Walters, Stanislav Kolibal, Marqueta Kolibal, Jan de Jong, Anne Clarke, Miranda Davies, and Hilary Arnold.

This book is dedicated to Eric Ayers.

EDITED BY JULIAN ROTHENSTEIN & MEL GOODING

FEATURES

INTRODUCTION

MEL GOODING

The letter, as an abstract written sign, developed from the pictogram, the simple drawing that accompanied speech into the making of the first human culture. The sign must exist, drawn by the finger in sand, marked in ash or ochre on the cave wall, scratched into clay by a stick, before the sound can be attached to it. "All letters began as signs," wrote Victor Hugo, "and all signs began as images." In a famous and not entirely fanciful little essay, the great novelist found in the modern alphabet everything from the image of man's simplest shelter to the portent of his destiny and the sign of God:

A is the roof, the gable with its crossbeam, the arch; or it is two friends greeting, who embrace and shake hands; D is the human back; B is the back on the back, the hump; C is the crescent, the moon; E is the foundations, the pillar, the console and the architrave, all architecture in a single letter; F is the gibbet; G is the French horn; H is a facade with two towers; I is the war machine launching its projectile; J is the plowshare and the horn of plenty; K is the angle of reflection equal to the angle of incidence, a key to geometry; L is the leg and foot; M is a mountain or a camp with tents pitched in pairs; N is a gate with a diagonal bar; O is the sun; P is a porter with a load on his back; Q is a rump with a tail; R is the porter resting on his staff; S is a serpent; T is a hammer; U is the urn, V the vase, which are easily confused; (Y is a tree, a fork, the confluence of two rivers, a stemmed glass, a man with arms up-stretched); X is crossed swords, a battle: who will win we do not know, so the mystics made it the sign of destiny and the algebraists the sign of the unknown; Z is lightning, the sign of God: That is what the alphabet contains.

10

There is indeed something quite magical about the look of the alphabet: it has to do with its infinite capacity to change shape and style, to express purpose and suggest mood, to be formal and informal, elegant and ugly, classical and romantic, delicate and robust. Every alphabet presents an orchestration of the letters to the eye, is a kind of score, a systematic optical abstract, a visual matrix out of which any number of possible messages might be composed. This visual versatility is, of course, directly related to the uses to which letters are put, and the form and nature of any message will depend on the type and scale of the lettering.

In this book, for example, there is reproduced, for the first time since their publication, a series of sign-writers' alphabets intended to find their public realization on shop fronts and bar signs; there are eye charts for the optician's patient; there are letters and signs for technical manuals; there is fine typography for beautiful books; there is a magisterial constructivist visual ballet; and so on. Every task demands its own kind of alphabet; every new purpose evolves its appropriate new lettering: of the making of alphabets there is no end.

We live in an age in which the use of letters, and recourse to diverse alphabets, is unprecedented, and in which more alphabets have been invented than ever before in history. In the period of modernism, whose progressive and humane principles we celebrate in this book, there was access as never before to good design and visual diversity. In magazines and books, on book jackets and film posters, in the packaging of goods and the advertisement of services, on buildings and in the streets, wherever information was conveyed there was evidence of the most intelligent and aesthetically sophisticated combination of utility and beauty.

The focus of this book, though not exclusively so, is on those alphabets, signs, designs, and diverse printed materials of the modern era that embody the optimistic modernist spirit of the early and mid-twentieth century. Beyond that, it has no program, and it makes no systematic presentation: it reflects the taste of the editors, their predilection for the wayward as well as for the rigorous in matters of design and typography. It is a book made for all lovers of letters and signs, for their use and for their delight.

THE ALPHABET

GEORGES PEREC

I have several times asked myself what logic was applied in the distribution of the six vowels and twenty consonants of our alphabet. Why start with A, then B, then C, etc.?

The fact that there is obviously no answer to this question is initially reassuring: the order of the alphabet is arbitrary, impressive, and therefore neutral. Objectively speaking, A is no better than B, the ABC is not a sign of excellence but only of a beginning (the ABC of one's métier).

But the mere fact that there is an order no doubt means that, sooner or later and more or less, each element in the series becomes the insidious bearer of a qualitative coefficient. Thus a B movie will be thought of as "less good" than another film, which, as it happens, no one has yet thought of calling an "A movie." Just as a cigarette manufacturer who has the words "Class A" stamped on his packets is giving us to understand that his cigarettes are superior to others.

The qualitative alphabetical code is not very well stocked. In fact, it has hardly more than three elements:

A = excellent

B = less good

Z = hopeless

But this doesn't stop it being a code and superimposing a whole hierarchical system on a sequence that is by definition inert.

For reasons that are somewhat different but still germane to my purpose, it may be noted that numerous companies go out of their way in their corporate titles to end up with acronyms of the AAA, ABC, AAAc, etc. kind so as to figure among the first entries in professional directories and phone books. Conversely, a schoolboy does well to have a name whose initial letter comes in the middle of the alphabet because he will then stand a better chance of not being asked a question.

from *Penser/Classer* (Think/Classify)

The types are *NOT* arranged in
alphabetical order

A

a

ABRICOT

APRICOT

APRIKOSE

G. KARQUEL ★ ALPHABET PHOTOGRAPHI

A B C D E F

G H J K L M

N O P Q R S

T U V X Y Z

SS

GB

SC

ET

BBS

MODÈLES DE

MW

FE

JEAN PUIFORCAT

SA

ME

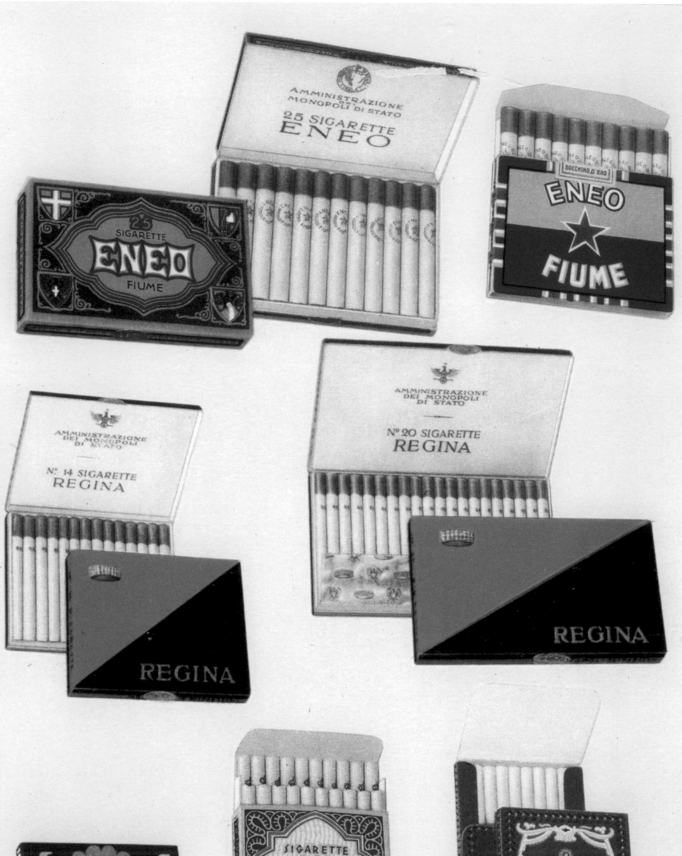

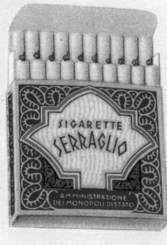

TIPPLER

Dusk to Dawn in the life of a Man-about-town, as shown by twenty-six different scenes, each decorating a letter of this tippler alphabet.

A B C D

E F G H I

J K L M

N O P Q R

S T U V

W X Y Z

TOME 1

DIVERTISSEMENTS TYPOGRAPHIQUES

TRAVAUX DE VILLE

ABCDEFG
HIJKLMN,
OPQRST.
UVWXYZ!
1234567890
abcdefgghij
klmnopqrst
uvwxyÿyz.&!

त

तरबूज

श

थरमस

द

दवात

दवात

ab

bbcddeef

ghᏟhrijkklꭲn

naꝑꝑꝗꝗꝛꝛss

otuvꝏᏔxꝗyyzo

3039

3040

3041

le mot.

Nº 2. — 1re Année.   10 Centimes   Lundi 7 Déc. 1914.

LOHENGRIN ET L'ÉCREVISSE

DESSIN DE PAUL IRIBE

LA MARCHE SUR PARIS.

144 Point
Ludlow 6-EC Gothic Extra Condensed

ABCDEF

GHIJKLM

NOPQRST

UVWX

> **NOTE**
> For the remainder of this alphabet, points, figures, other characters, information, etc., see the following page

Y Z & 1 2 3 4

5 6 7 8 9 0 $

£ . : , - ' ? !

SINCLAIR

MACHT MAN DOLLARS

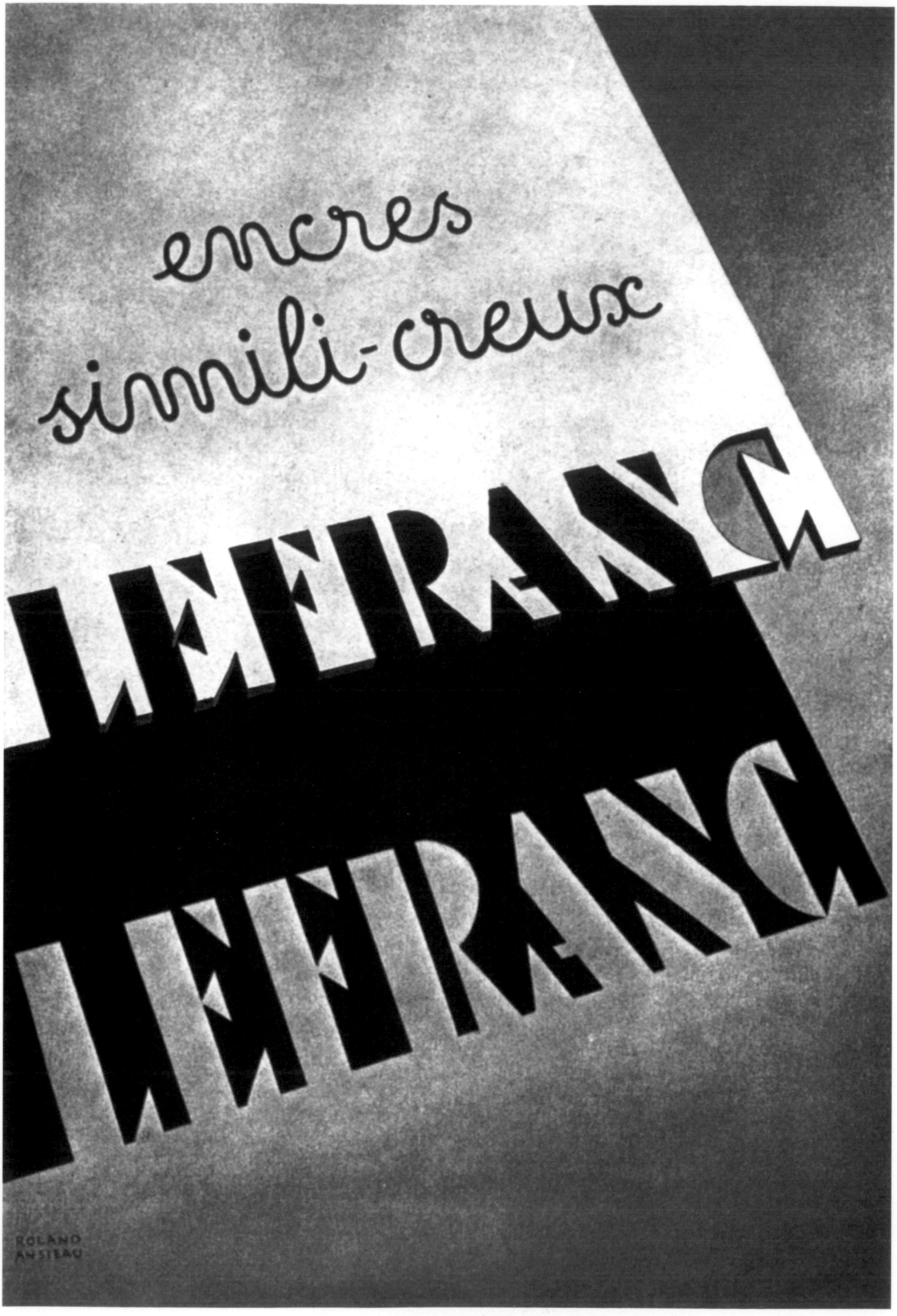
encres
simili-creux
LEFRANC
LEFRANC
ROLAND
ANSIEAU

ABCDEFG

HIJKLŁM

NOPRST

U·W·Y·Z

·1234567890·

Diese Schablonenschrift ist aus typographischem Material (Messinglinien) entstanden und kann, wie in den hier gezeigten Beispielen 1, 2, 3, systematisch breiter oder höher gemacht werden

Kunstgewerbeschule Stuttgart (Walter Veit). Schablonenschrift

KONSTRUIERTE SCHRIFTEN

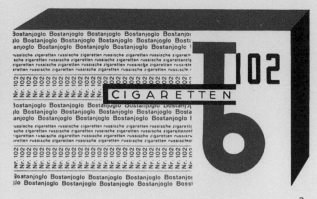

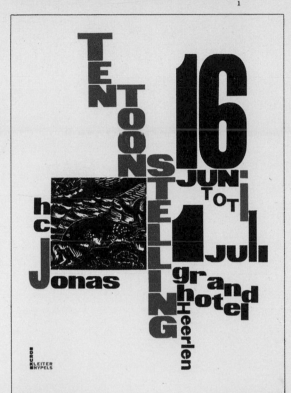

1, Franz Stautner, Mannheim. Geschäftskarte der Buchdruckerei G. Jacob, Mannheim. 2, Grete Stern, Stuttgart. Cigaretten-packung. 3, Buchdruckerei C. Nypels, Maastricht. Plakat für eine Kunstausstellung. 4, Erich Matthes, Erasmus-Druck, Berlin. Anzeige für MK-Papier. 5, 7, Nicolai Ilijin, Nishnij-Nowgorod. Zwei Buchumschläge. 6, Unbek. Buchumschlag

TYPOGRAPHISCHE BEISPIELE

JAPANESE OLD ORIENTAL DINNERWARE EXOTIC KIMONOS PAPER KITES TIES

天回來他若今天不來呢那怎麼樣○有人說山西反了○這個事情

CHINESE IS BEST SEE LEFT TO RIGHT, BUT VERTICAL READING IS QUITE AUTHENTIC

A B C D E F G H H
I I I J K L U M N N O
M P P R S S T U U V
W X Y Z 1 2 3 4 5 6 7 8 9 0

33

Photo Finsler, 1933: BAG 16 (Wandlampe mit Gleitschuh)

KUPFERTIEFDRUCK BÜCHLER & CO. BERN

ЖЕЛЕЗНОДОРОЖНИК ПОМНИ
БЕСПЕРЕБОЙНЫЕ ПЕРЕВОЗКИ ОСНОВА
УСПЕШНОГО ВЫПОЛНЕНИЯ ПЯТИЛЕТКИ
НАРОДНОГО ХОЗЯЙСТВА В ЧЕТЫРЕ ГОДА

Д.БУЛАНОВ

ПЯТИЛЕТКА КАДРОВ ОБЩЕСТВЕННОГО ПИТАНИЯ

НАРПИТОВЕЦ ПОВЫШАЙ СВОЮ КВАЛИФИКАЦИЮ

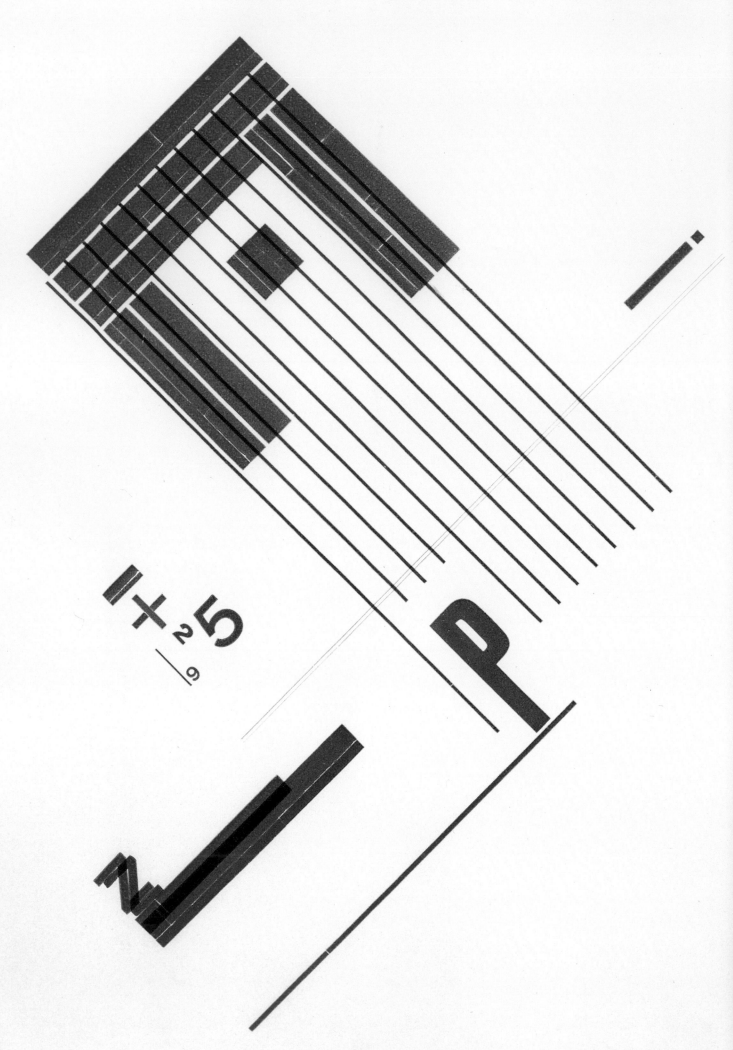

A CZECH MODERNIST ALPHABET

Karel Teige (1900–1951) was the greatest of the Czech avant-garde artist-writers of the 1920s and 1930s. His 1926 photomontage designs for the twenty-four-poem sequence *Abeceda*, written by his friend Víteslav Nezval, are a uniquely elegant and witty invention, one of the enduring achievements of Czech modernism. The designs feature the third collaborator in the project, the dancer Milca Mayarová, whose idea it was to choreograph the poems, creating a pose for each letter, and then to publish the book with Teige's title designs. Using Karel Paspa's photographs of Mayarová, which contrive to be both erotic and chastely gymnastic, Teige's designs transform the alphabet into what is effectively a constructivist manifesto, a demonstration of his aim to create a new "optical language, a system of signs capable of embodying words in graphic figures." It is a stunning realization of what László Moholy-Nagy had called for in his influential 1925 Bauhaus book, *Painting, Photography, Film,* the dynamic combination of photographic image and lettering he termed "typofoto." Like Mayarová, Teige succeeds in finding an utterly original and distinctive solution for every letter: her brilliant pose alphabet is animated into a visual dance, what Nezval called "a living poem."

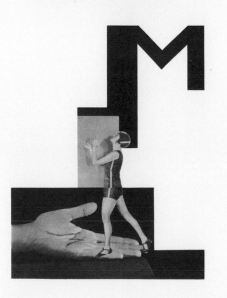

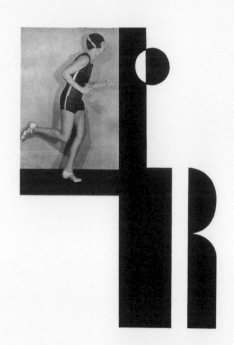

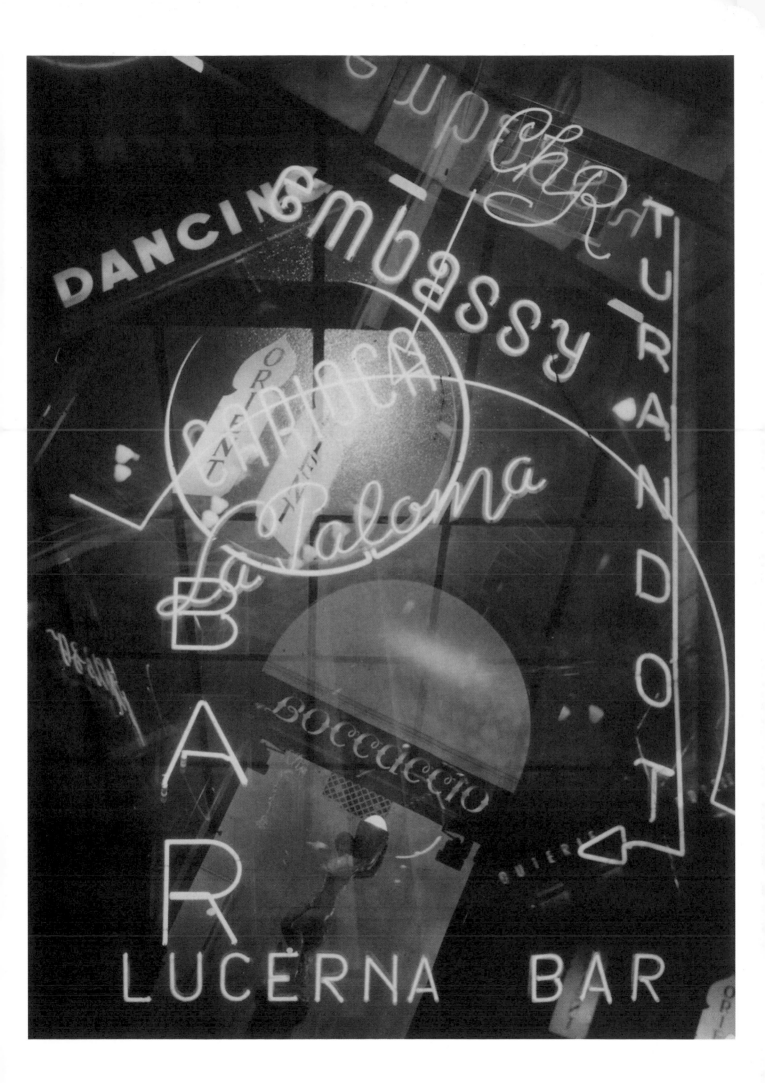

ABCDEF
GHIJKLM
NOPQRST
UVWXYZ

Rotterdamsche Schilderschool,
A. R. VAN DER BURG

A. R. VAN DER BURG.

ABCDEF
GHIJKLM
NOPQRST
UVWXYZ

Rotterdamsche Schilderschool,
A. R. VAN DER BURG.

A. R. VAN DER BURG.

abcdefghij
klmnopqr
stuvwxyz
1234567890

Rotterdamsche Schilderschool,
A. R. VAN DER BURG.

A. R. VAN DER BURG.

abcdefghi
jklmnopqr
stuvwxyz
1234567890

Rotterdamsche Schilderschool,
A. R. VAN DER BURG

A. R. VAN DER BURG.

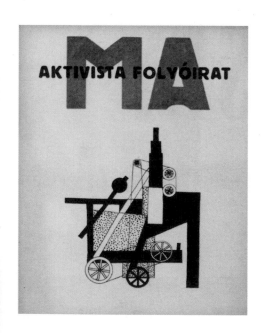

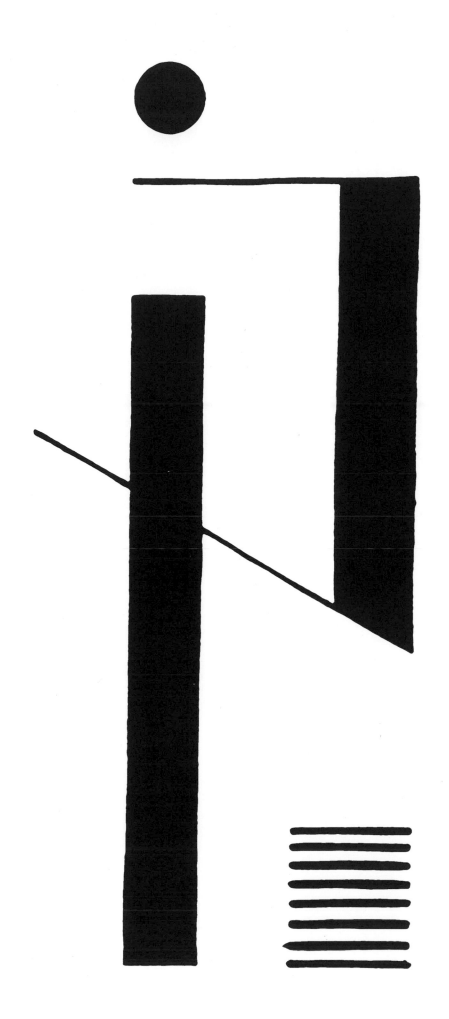

Publicité Dam.

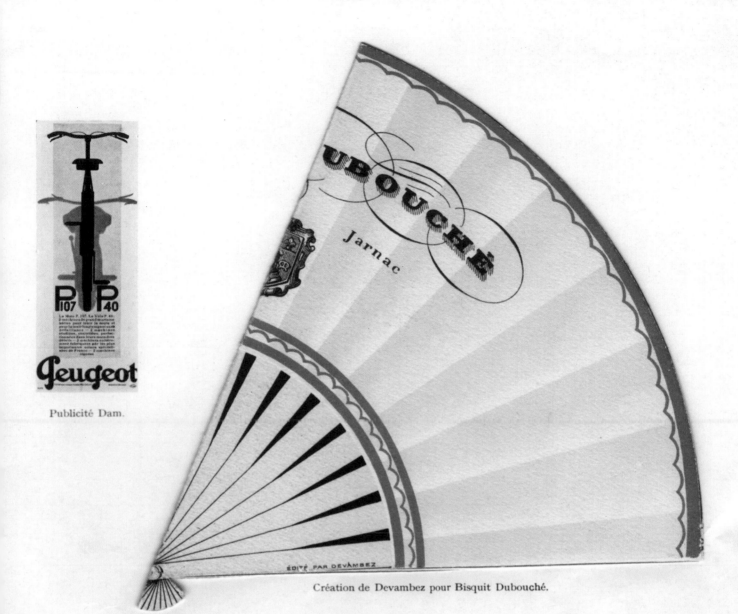

Création de Devambez pour Bisquit Dubouché.

Annonce pour les montres Lip.

Page d'annonce (Édit. Paul-Martial).

Dessin de Francis Bernard
(Édit. Paul-Martial).

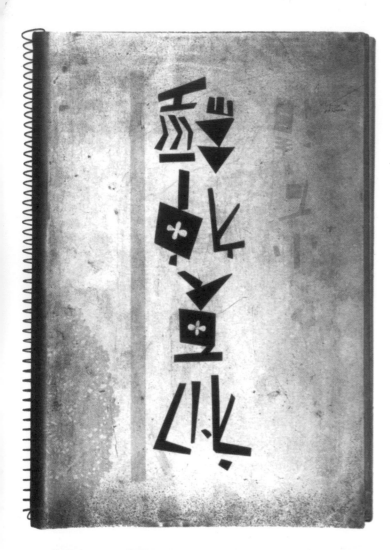

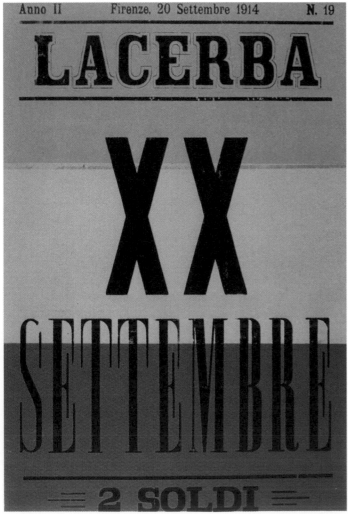

LICHTDRUCK

ELEMENTARE
TYPOGRAPHIE
MIT
ERBAR
GROTESK
SCHRIFTEN
DER
SCHRIFTGIESSEREI
LUDWIG & MAYER
FRANKFURT
AM MAIN

BEILAGE ZUR „GEBRAUCHSGRAPHIK"
ENTWURF, SATZ UND DRUCK
KÖLNER WERKSCHULEN
KLASSE ERBAR

Welche erfreuliche Veränderung zeigt sich schon seit zwei Jahrzehnten auf dem Gebiete der Schriftschneidekunst, gegenüber der Verflachung des Geschmackes in den letzten Jahrzehnten vorigen Jahrhunderts! Wir haben eine große Zahl von Antiquaschriften erhalten, die einen so hohen Grad der Durchgeistigung zeigen, daß sie den besten alten Vorbildern der Zeit des handwerklichen Schaffens an die Seite gestellt werden können.

Nur bei einer Schriftart, den Grotesk-Schriften, war seither von dem frischen Zug, der durch das Kunstgewerbe geht, nichts zu verspüren Die Grotesk-Schriften hat man wohl in allen möglichen Breiten und Fetten gebracht, aber eine künstlerische Neugestaltung der Formen hat man unterlassen.

Man glaubte nach klassischen Vorbildern zu arbeiten und hat nur den Ungeschmack in eine verfeinerte Form gebracht, dadurch, daß man die langweilige Eintönigkeit noch peinlicher unterstrich.

EIN VIERTEL
JAHRHUNDERT
DRUCKFARBEN
FABRIKEN
GEBR. HARTMANN
HALLE-AMMENDORF

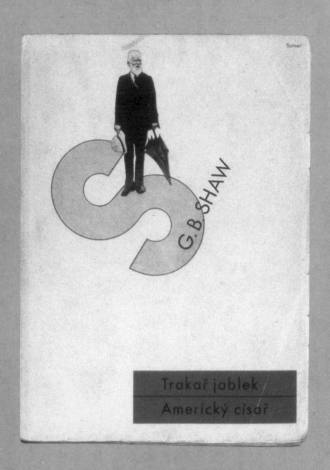

G. B. SHAW

Trakař jablek

Americký císař

G. B. SHAW

Člověk nikdy neví

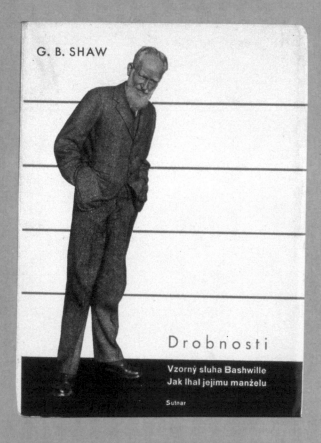

G. B. SHAW

Drobnosti

Vzorný sluha Bashwille

Jak lhal jejimu manželu

Sutnar

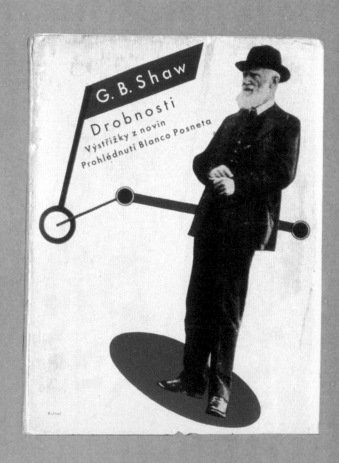

G. B. Shaw

Drobnosti

Výstřižky z novin

Prohlédnutí Blanco Posneta

HÁNOSŮĚBL
JĎDCKMPRW
ČVXZYÍFT

nahebydskr
ctmfjópžgvl
wxž2345678u

abdeghk
npqc uv

mu dos
xyzfijrtl

ABCDEEF
GHIJKLM
TOPQRS
U8VWX
YZ

DIE CENCI

ZEITSCHRIFT DES VERBANDES

DERRIAME

1.JULIHEFT 1927
HEFT №13
E.V.
DEUTSCHER REKLAMEFACHLEUTE

PABLO PICASSO
PICASSO

WORTH
7. RUE DE LA PAIX

DEUTSCHE
OPAK
GLAS
WERKE

RUSCHEWEYH
MÖBEL

RUSCHEWEYH
TISCHE

a b c d e f g h i j k l m n o
p q r f s t u v w x y z
A B C D E F G H I J K L M N
O P Q R S T U V W X Y Z

KONSTRUIERTE SCHRIFTEN

Geschäftsbücherfabrik & Druckerei
Dietz & Lüchtrath A·G
MÜNCHEN

BUCH
STEIN
OFFSET
VIERFARBENDRUCK

VORNEHME WERBEDRUCKE

Lettres majuscules.

ABCDE
FGHIJK
LMNOP
QRSTU
VWXYZ

ABCDEFG
HIJKLMN
OPQRST
UVWXYZ
abcdefghij
klmnopqrst
uvwxyzæœ

MILANO

HOOGST
SLOEG HET
„BERKEL" WEDSTRIJD 1 JAN.–30 JUNI 1928
HY
A. BOTERMANS Jr. 141,3 %
J. C. KOOPMAN 141,- %
E. ROMEIJN 124,- %
D. DIJKSTRA 121,9 %
W. LEGERSTEE 121,6 %
G. DIEPENHEIM 118,2 %
J. REBEL 113,9 %
H. G. BOTERMANS 110,3 %
H. HENNINK 106,9 %
A. VAN VELZEN 102,1 %
A. NOORDHOFF 98,- %
M. DERKSEN 96,6 %
A. BAMMENS 94,7 %
C. VAN HOLST 92,9 %
W. DE HAAS 90,- %
F. GOOSEN 87,5 %
H. J. F. KIECKENS 82,3 %
D. VAN BELLE 82,5 %
A. VOGEL 80,1 %
D. VISSER 73,7 %
H. VAN BOSSUM SR. 68.3%
STAND OP 1 JUNI
RECLAME PAUL SCHUITEMA

ABCD
EFGHI
KLMN
OPQR
STUV
WXYZ

XXe SIECLE No 4
XXth CENTURY
XX
ÉDITION IN ENGLISH
CHRISTMAS 1938

THE ANTIFASCIST SCHOOLBOOK

In 1937 the republican government of Spain was deeply embroiled in the savage civil war against the fascist rebellion led by General Franco. Under the leadership of the minister of education, Jesús Hernández, the Ministry of Public Information issued *Cartilla Escolar Antifascista*, a literacy primer, as an aid to the campaign of the "cultural militias" against illiteracy. The booklet, beautifully designed by Mauricio Amster, who also created the poster advertising the "schoolbook," combined phonetics with politics, identifying the military struggle against fascism with the cultural fight against ignorance. Pages from this poignant document are reproduced here for the first time since its publication in republican Spain's heroic years of travail and hope. The civil war ended in March 1939, with the final defeat of the republic.

¡VIVA MADRID HEROICO!

VI-VA MA-DRID HE-ROI-CO

Vi-va Ma-drid he-roi-co

i, a, e, o

V, v, M, d, r, h, c

ejemplos de sílabas:

Ha, he, hi, ho, hu, re, mos, na, Es,
Ha, he, hi, ho, hu, re, mos, na, Es,

As, Is, Os, Us, pa, ña, ñe, fe, fa, fi,
As, Is, Os, Us, pa, ña, ñe, fe, fa, fi,

fo, fu, lir, lar, lur.
fo, fu, lir, lar, lur.

ejemplos de palabras:

Hacer, hago, haces, hacemos, hágamos, haréis, hacían,
Hacer, hago, haces, hacemos, hágamos, haréis, hacían,

hecho, haber, hiena, hierro, honda, hospital, huelga,
hecho, haber, hiena, hierro, honda, hospital, huelga.

Esteban, Ismael, fosa, fusil, feroz.
Esteban, Ismael, fosa, fusil, feroz.

Nuestros combatientes luchan como
Nuestros combatientes luchan como

héroes.
héroes.

JESUS HERNANDEZ, NUESTRO MINISTRO DE INSTRUCCION

Je-sús Her-nán-dez, nues-tro
Mi-nis-tro de Ins-truc-ción.

J-e-s-ú-s H-e-r-n-á-n-d-e-z, n-u-e-s-t-r-o
M-i-n-i-s-t-r-o d-e I-n-s-t-r-u-c-c-i-ó-n.

i, e, u, a, o
J, s, H, r, n, d, z, M, I.

SOLIDARIDAD INTERNACIONAL

So-li-da-ri-dad in-ter-na-cio-nal

o, i, a,

Tra, Tre, Tri, Tro, Tru, ba, be, je,
Tra, Tre, Tri, Tro, Tru, ba, be, je,

ja, ji, jo, ju, mos, mas, pa, pe, ra,
ja, ji, jo, ju, mos, mas, pa, pe, ra,

la, gue, gui, güe, güi, rra, rre.
la, gue, gui, güe, güi, rra, rre,

tropas, ultraje, jovial, agujero, jugo, racimo, ración,
tropas, ultraje, jovial, agujero, jugo, racimo, ración,

trinchera, Trubia, ametralladora, traje, ajetreo, trigo,
trinchera, Trubia, ametralladora, traje, ajetreo, trigo,

barra, rojo, jarra, jara, reloj, aparejo, guijarro,
barra, rojo, jarra, jara, reloj, aparejo, guijarro

pingüe, argüir.
pingüe, argüir,

La juventud gloriosa se bate en
La juventud gloriosa se bate en

las trincheras.
las trincheras.

REPUBLICA DEMOCRATICA

RE-PU-BLI-CA DE-MO-CRA-TI-CA

R-e-p-ú-b-l-i-c-a d-e-m-o-c-r-á-t-i-c-a

e, u, i, a, o

R, p, b, l, c, d, m, r, t

LENIN, NUESTRO GRAN MAESTRO

Le-nin, nues-tro gran ma-es-tro

e, i, u, o, a

L, n, s, t, r, g, m

AÑO IV - NUMERO 3 (20) MAYO - JUNIO 1953

SIN⊕SIS

R E V I S T A   M E D I C A

EDITADA POR "ESTABLECIMIENTOS MEXICANOS COLLIERE, S. A."

ATAVIOS DE LOS DIOSES.—*Códice matritense del Real Palacio.*

ARTE PREHISPANICO por *Vladimiro Rosado Ojeda*, pág. 19

EXPOSITION D'ART MEXICAIN
ANCIEN ET MODERNE

MUSÉE NATIONAL D'ART MODERNE
PARIS · MAI-JUILLET 1952

MEXICO en el ARTE
número 12

OPERA
NACIONAL
con la COLABORACION del INBA
1951

TRATAMIENTO DEL ALCOHOLISMO

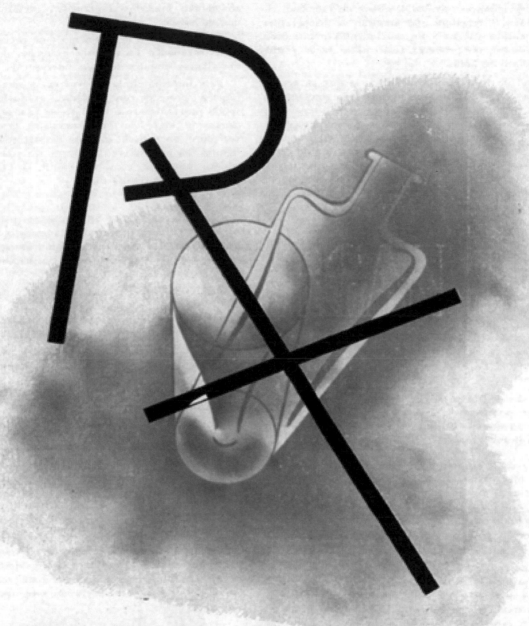

Etabus

aaaaaa bbbb c

ddefgghij

klmnooopp

qqrrʃstuv

wxxyz

А. Крученых

ЕЖИПТИЕН

А Б В Г

Д Е Ж З И

К Л М Н О

П Р С Т У Ф Х

Ц Ч Ш Щ

Ъ Ь Ю Я

---

1 2 3 4 5 6 7

8 9 & 9 0

ABCDEFGHIJ
KĹMNOPQRS
TUVXYZW !?

PRÍLOHA 1
Pražský grotesk

АБВГГДЕДЖЗИЙК
ЛЛМНОПРСТУФХ
ЦЧШЩЭЮЯЯЁЬЫЬЪ

PRÍLOHA 2
Azbuka úzka

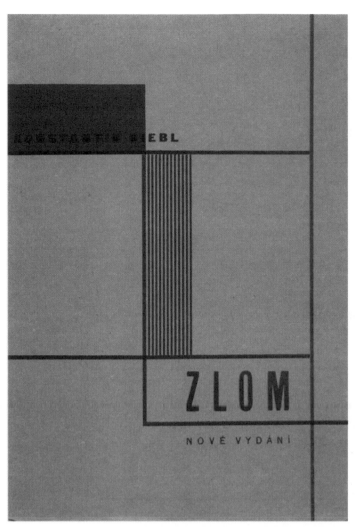

KONSTANTIN BIEBL

ZLOM

NOVÉ VYDÁNÍ

BÁSEŇ
NOCI 5.
SVAZEK
EDICE
OLYMP
PRAHA
1 9 2 6

diabolo

Vítězslav Nezval

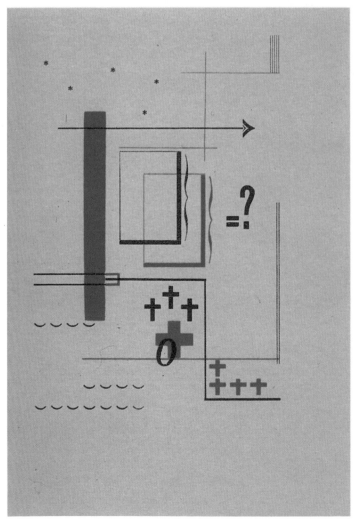

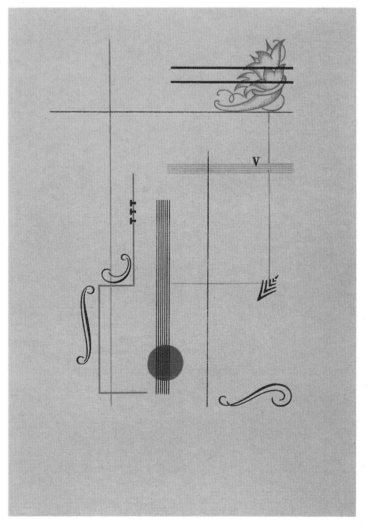

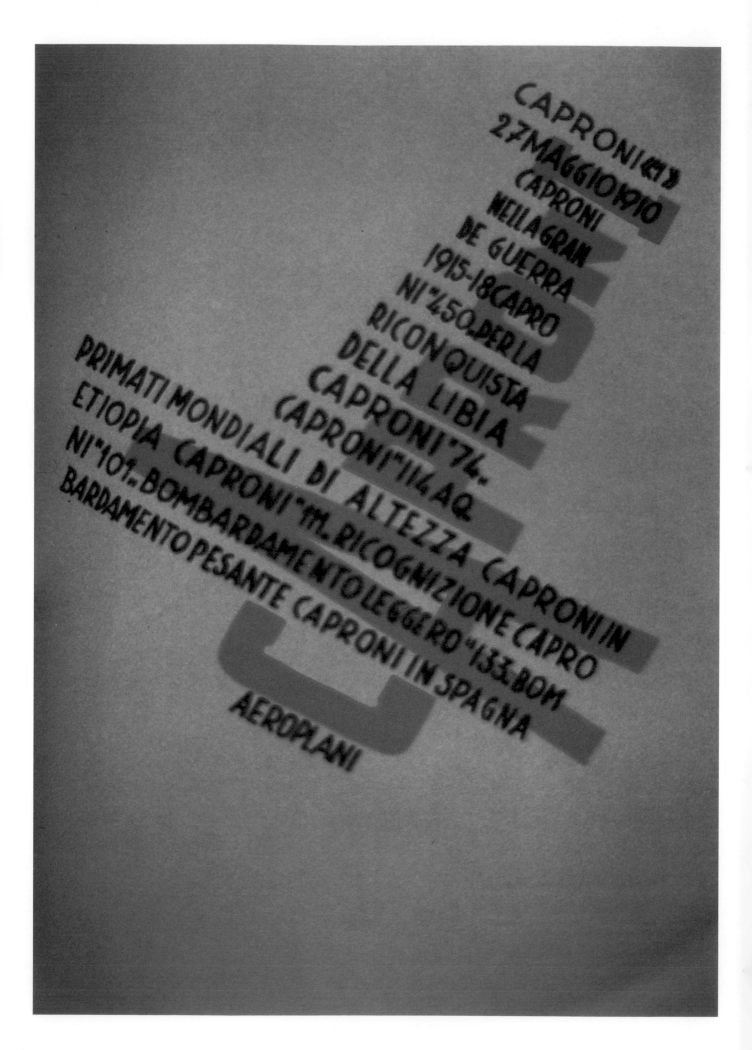

CAPRONI «1»

27 MAGGIO 1910

CAPRONI NELLA GRAN DE GUERRA 1915-18 CAPRO NI "450" PER LA RICONQUISTA DELLA LIBIA CAPRONI "74." CAPRONI "114 AQ

PRIMATI MONDIALI DI ALTEZZA CAPRONI IN ETIOPIA CAPRONI "m. RICOGNIZIONE CAPRO NI "101" BOMBARDAMENTO LEGGERO "133. BOM BARDAMENTO PESANTE CAPRONI IN SPAGNA

AEROPLANI

ABCDEFI

GHJKLM

NOPQRW

STUVYXZ

abcdefg
hijklno
mpqrſw
stuvxyz

FRANCISCONI

CAMPO
GRAFICO

RIVISTA DI ESTETICA E DI TECNICA GRAFICA · MILANO · NUMERO 1 · GENNAIO 1939 · SPEDIZ. IN ABBON. POSTALE

ABCDE
FGHIJK
LMNOP
QRSTU
VWXYZ
&$!?&&
12345
67890

ИЛЬЯ ЗДАНЕВИЧ
зохна и женихи

le mot.

N° 17. — 1ʳᵉ Année. 30 Centimes. Samedi 1ᵉʳ Mai 1915.

DESSIN DE PAUL IRIBE.

LA VEILLÉE DES NEUTRES.

HNBDICRMKE

GOPÁVSYŮWL

JŠTZXFMYJQ

1234567890 2

abrphxfcvdn.

stgmjúyeikz

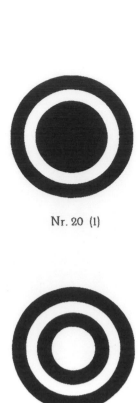

Nr. 20 (1)

Nr. 25 (4)

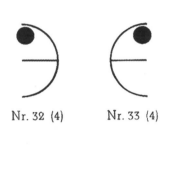

Nr. 30 (2)

Nr. 21 (1)

Nr. 26 (2)

Nr. 31 (2)

Nr. 22 (1)

Nr. 27 (2)

Nr. 32 (4)   Nr. 33 (4)

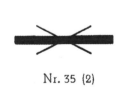

Nr. 34 (4)

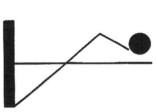

Nr. 23 (1)

Nr. 28 (2)

Nr. 35 (2)

Nr. 24 (2)

Nr. 29 (2)

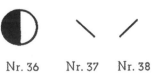

Nr. 36   Nr. 37   Nr. 38

Einfassung 1 m

abcdefghijk
œlmnopqrstuy
wxz
xyz

Crous-Vidal, dont l'exposition à la Galerie
d'Orsay fut le "clou" graphique de la ren-
trée 52, a dédié à Jean Giono et à l'école de
Lure ce flamboyant caractère d'inspiration
méditerranènne :
LES CATALANES

LES CATALANES

ISCANRD123
FGHJKLMOPTUV

TWO SIMPLE STEPS TO STENCIL MARKING

1
CUT THE STENCIL

Slip in a sheet of stencil board—turn the wheel—press the handle. In a minute or less you have cut a stencil—clean, accurate.

Operators soon learn to cut stencils on the Marsh Machine with lightning speed because of the improved features shown on pages 20 and 21.

2
MARK THE SHIPMENT

Lay the stencil on the shipment—make a few strokes with the Marsh Fountain Brush and you have a stencil mark—water-proof, smear-proof, permanent.

Marsh inks made in block and various colors for marking boxes, cartons, metal, all kinds of shipments are shown on pages 26 to 29.

No. 1 Office, Shipping Dept. Assembly Dept.
No. 2 Machine Shop, Ink Dept. Oil Board Dept.
No. 3 Warehouse, Raw Material Storage.

J. W. MARSH
1869—1935
Founder

WALT MARSH
President

E. J. MARSH
Sec'y & Treas.

PAUL WAGNER
Ass't Treas. & Legal Counsel

HERBERT W. HEMPEL
Chief Engineer

FRED BUCHMANN
Plant Supt.

MARSH

MOST men set out to make their mark in the world. Marsh of Belleville was different. He set out to help other men make their marks.

Yes, the most legible marks of all—STENCIL MARKS. Neat, bold, attractive, permanent. Marks that say: "This shipment is from a firm that's proud of its product, service, reputation."

From the Marsh Factory flow the stencil machines, brushes, inks, stencil board to serve industry and transportation, to aid business—free enterprise—in its task of serving all the people.

MARSH STENCIL MACHINE COMPANY
BELLEVILLE, ILLINOIS, U. S. A.

U. S. AGENCIES	DENVER	MINNEAPOLIS	ST. LOUIS	FOREIGN AGENCIES	INDIA
ATLANTA	DETROIT	NASHVILLE	ST. PAUL	ARGENTINA	MEXICO
BALTIMORE	DULUTH	NEW HAVEN	SALT LAKE	AUSTRALIA	NETHERLANDS
BIRMINGHAM	EL PASO	NEW ORLEANS	SAN ANTONIO	BELGIUM	NEWFOUNDLAND
BOISE	FORT WORTH	NEW YORK CITY	SAN FRANCISCO	BRAZIL	NORWAY
BOSTON	HARTFORD	OMAHA	SEATTLE	CANADA	PHILIPPINE ISLANDS
BRIDGEPORT	HOUSTON	PHILADELPHIA	SPOKANE	CHILE	PORTO RICO
BUFFALO	KANSAS CITY	PHOENIX	SYRACUSE	COLOMBIA	SWEDEN
CHICAGO	LOS ANGELES	PITTSBURGH	TACOMA	CUBA	SWITZERLAND
CINCINNATI	LOUISVILLE	PORTLAND	TAMPA	ENGLAND	URUGUAY
CLEVELAND	MEMPHIS	PROVIDENCE	TOLEDO	FRANCE	UNION OF S. AFRICA
DALLAS	MILWAUKEE	ROCHESTER	WASHINGTON, D. C.	HAWAII	VENEZUELA

REPUTATION FOR LEADERSHIP IS EARNED BY YEARS OF TRUSTWORTHY PERFORMANCE

One bank of drilling spindles

Quality Control Inspection

Turning Die Carriers to size

Presses for high-speed production

Group of skilled Punch Fitters

Sales Dept. expedites orders

Dies finished for perfect accuracy

Making Stencil Ink—Black & Colors

Assembling the Marsh Fountain Brush

Assembling Marsh Stencil Machines

Final Inspection and Approval

On their way to serve and save

18

This is an actual reproduction of the stencil characters cut by Model S (¾" size) Marsh Stencil Machine.

Model S ¾" Machine cuts this size stencil, one to four lines, any length. For marking medium sized shipments. Size of Machine 21" x 16" x 10" high. Weight 100 lbs. Packed 145 lbs.

Size of Stencil Board for Model S ¾" Machine

1-line 3" x 20"   3-line 5" x 20"
2-line 4" x 20"   4-line 6" x 20"

3/4"

ABCDEFGHIJ
KLMNOPQRST
UVWXYZ'/&,
23456789-.

19

This is an actual reproduction of the stencil characters cut by the Model R (1" size) Marsh Stencil Machine.

Model R 1" Machine cuts this size, one to four lines, any length. For marking large shipments. Size of machine 24" x 18" x 10" high. Weight 145 lbs. Packed 195 lbs.

Size of Stencil Board for Model R 1" Machine.

1-line 4" x 20" or 24"   3-line 6" x 20" or 24"
2-line 5" x 20" or 24"   4-line 7" x 20" or 24"

1"

ABCDEFGHIJ
KLMNOPQRST
UVWXYZ'/&,
23456789-.

iiiiunmrccaoevwxzžsj

yqgpltdbhchkf

IHLFETJUCGOQXYVWŽŽ

I.II.V.X.   *AMNDPBRKS*   L.C.D.M.

1234567890.

Achilles, Tantalus, Palermo, Vesuv.

ABCČDEFGHIJKLMNOPQR
ŘSŠTUVWXYZŽ&
abcdefghijklmnopqrstuvwxyz
1234567890 I. II. III. IV. V. VI. VII. VIII. IX. X.

ABCČDEFGHIJKLMNOP
QRŘSŠTUVWXYZŽ&
abcdefghijklmnopqrstuvxyz
1234567890 I. II. III. IV. V. VI. VII. VIII. IX. X.

OT. ŠTORCH-MARIEN

KILIMA-NDŽARO LÁSKY

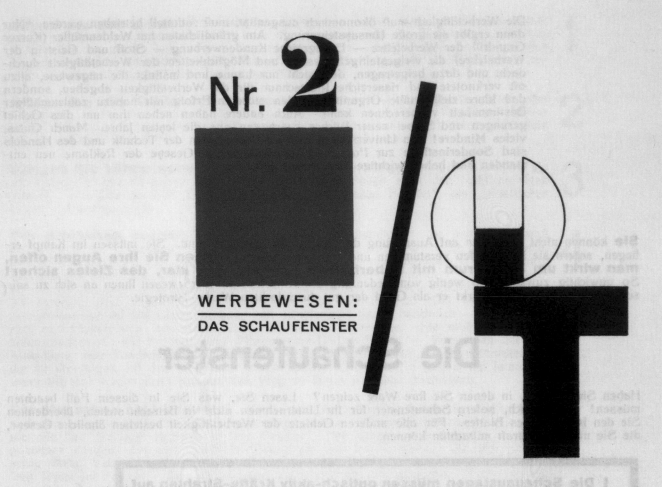

Nr. 2

WERBEWESEN:

DAS SCHAUFENSTER

„Sie können ruhig Ihren Mittagsschlaf sich gönnen!"

Organisieren Sie Ihre Werbetätigkeit! Die arbeitet für Sie und trägt Gewinn herein,
auch wenn Sie schlafen.

Flugblätter mit dem Buntquadrat
werden herausgegeben von Max Burchartz.
Sie erscheinen bei der Westdeutschen
Treuhandgesellschaft Canis & Co., K.-G.,
Bochum. Sie bringen Aufsätze (meist mit
Abbildungen) von Künstlern und Fachleuten
über allgemeine und besondere Fragen
der Kultur und Organisation, der Bau-
gestaltung, der Formgestaltung von Indu-
strieerzeugnissen und über Werbewesen.

Bewahren Sie jedes
„Flugblatt mit einem
Buntquadrat" gut auf!
Sehen Sie ab u. zu hin-
ein! Es bringt Ihnen Ge-
winn, sofern Sie seine
Ratschläge befolgen.

ABCDEFGHIJ
KLMNOPQR
STUVWXYZ

abcdefghijklm
nopqrstuvwxyz

werbe-entwurf
und ausführung

dessau, bauhaus
d

herbert-bayer
b

... das wesen ... einer aufgabe muß erforscht und erkannt werden, ... wird die äußere erscheinung einer werbsache das logische mittel sein zum zweck, den die werbsache erfüllen soll.   eine arbeit nach dieser auffassung verbürgt überzeugungskraft und qualität.   alle darstellungsmittel der typografie, fotografie, malerei, zeichnung . . . . ich zweckmäßig an bei: warenzeichen, geschäftspapier, ... prospekt, plakat, packung, werbebau und anderen werbsachen. ... ... kenntnisse und erfahrungen sichern eine wirtschaft- ...

vdr-kartei
werbindust
februar 19

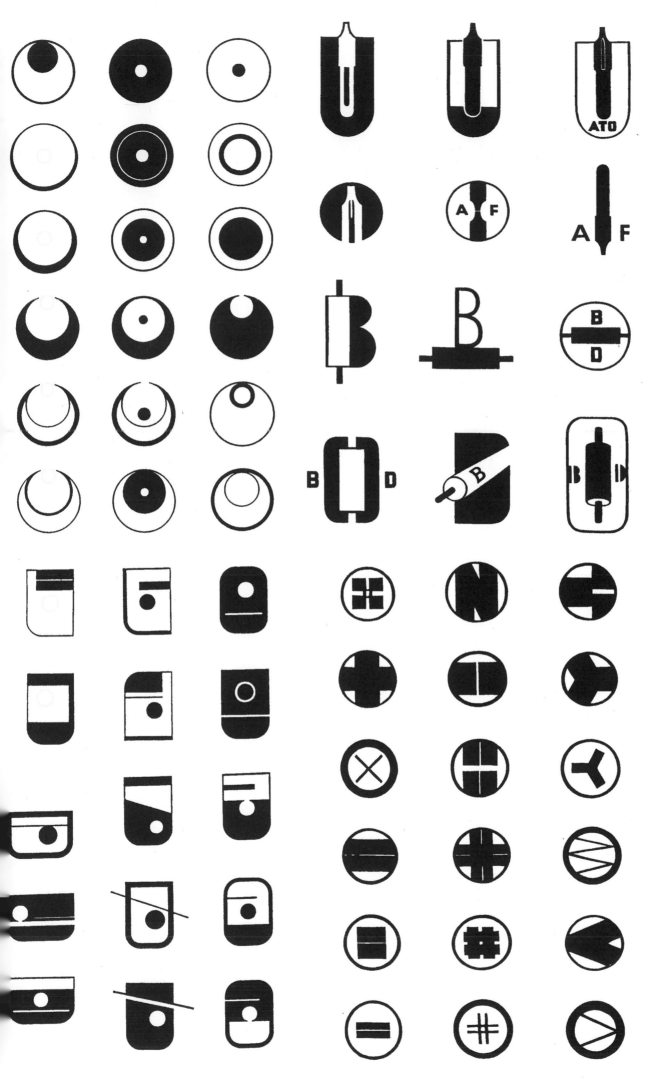

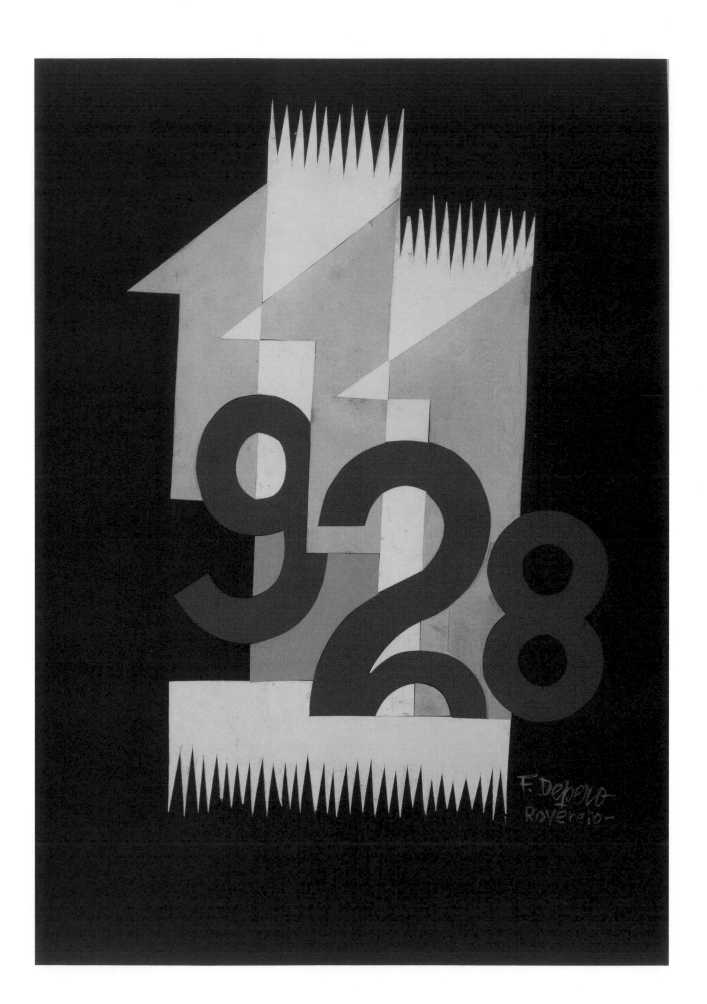

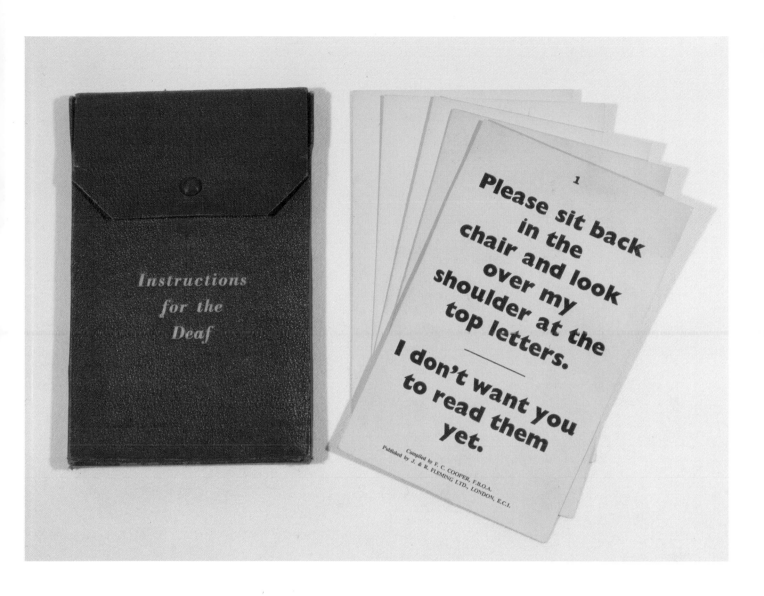

EYE TEST CHARTS

Eye test charts using letters of the alphabet, designed to test visual acuity and the efficacy of corrective lenses, were introduced in the 1830s. To increase optical distance in the testing room, some charts are designed with reversed letters and viewed through a facing mirror. In 1862 the Utrecht optometrist Herman Snellen designed the first scientifically reliable charts for testing vision distance, using carefully size-adjusted letters based on the typeface Egyptian Paragon. Sans-serif letters, having less visual distraction, were introduced soon after. (Gill Sans Bold has been especially popular with British opticians.) In the 1870s Snellen introduced charts with calibrated lines and abstract figures for young or illiterate patients. Eye test chart designs all over the world are still based on Snellen's pioneering "Optotypes." The economy and clarity demanded by its function gave the eye test chart a typographic formal elegance that was modernist avant la lettre.

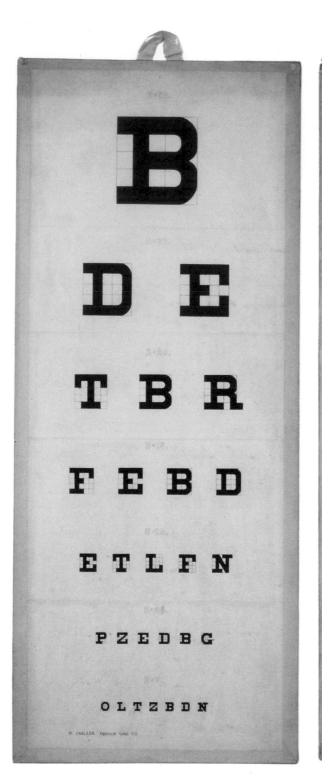
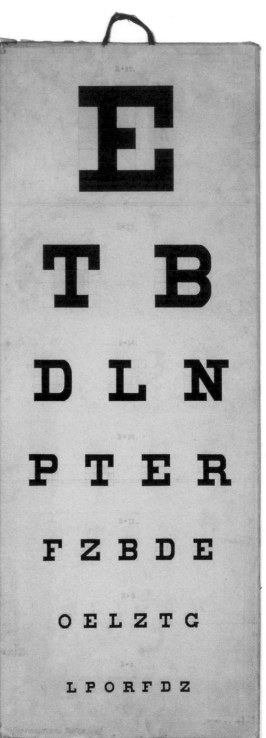

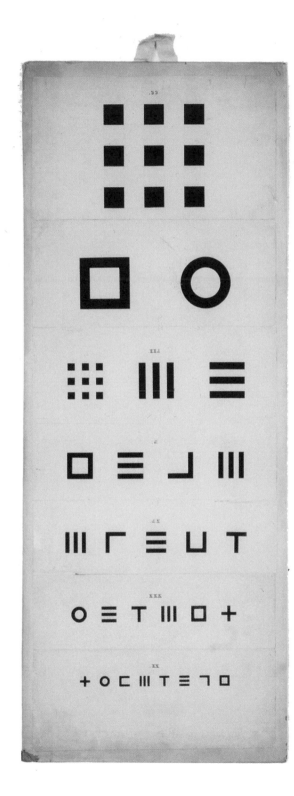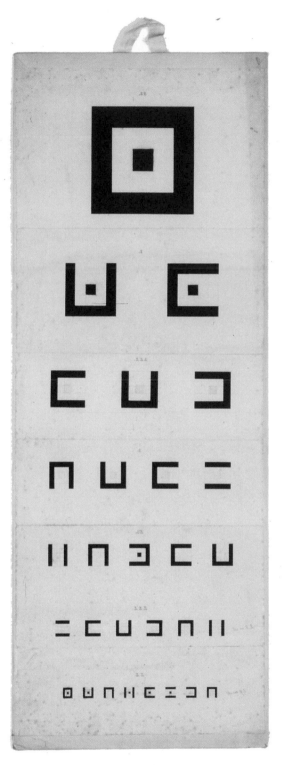

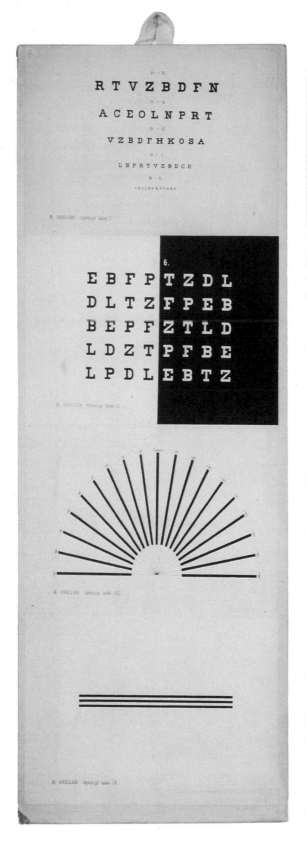

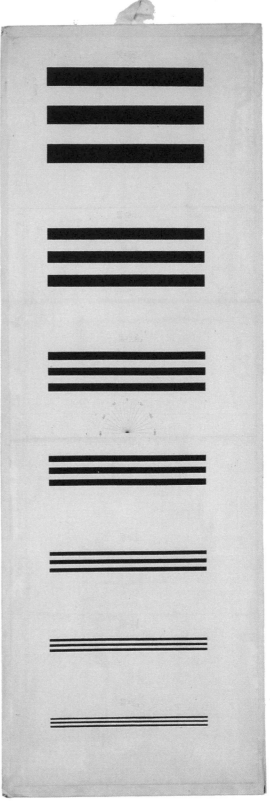

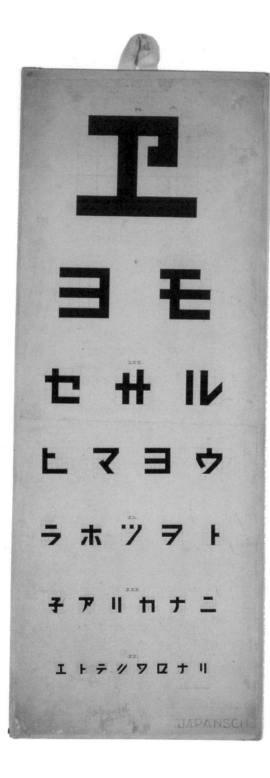

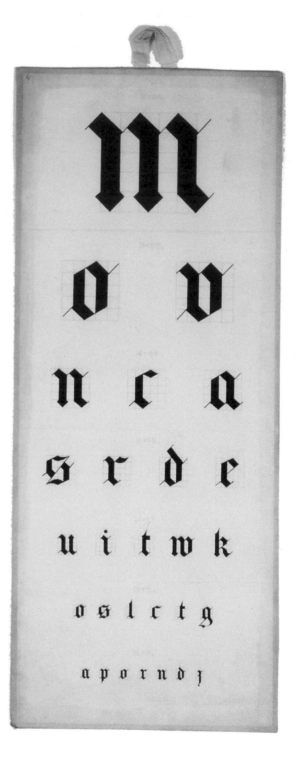

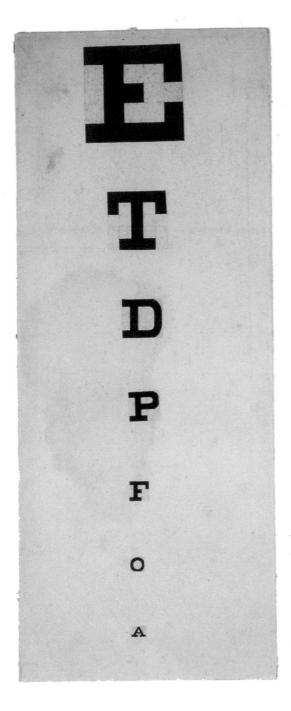
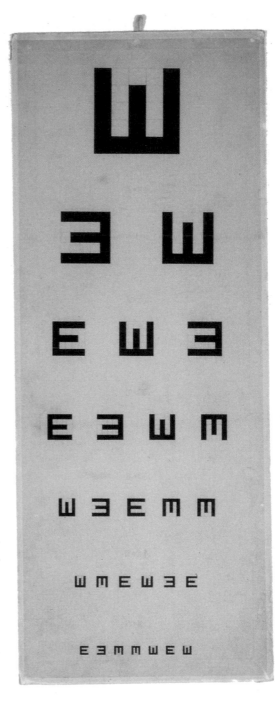

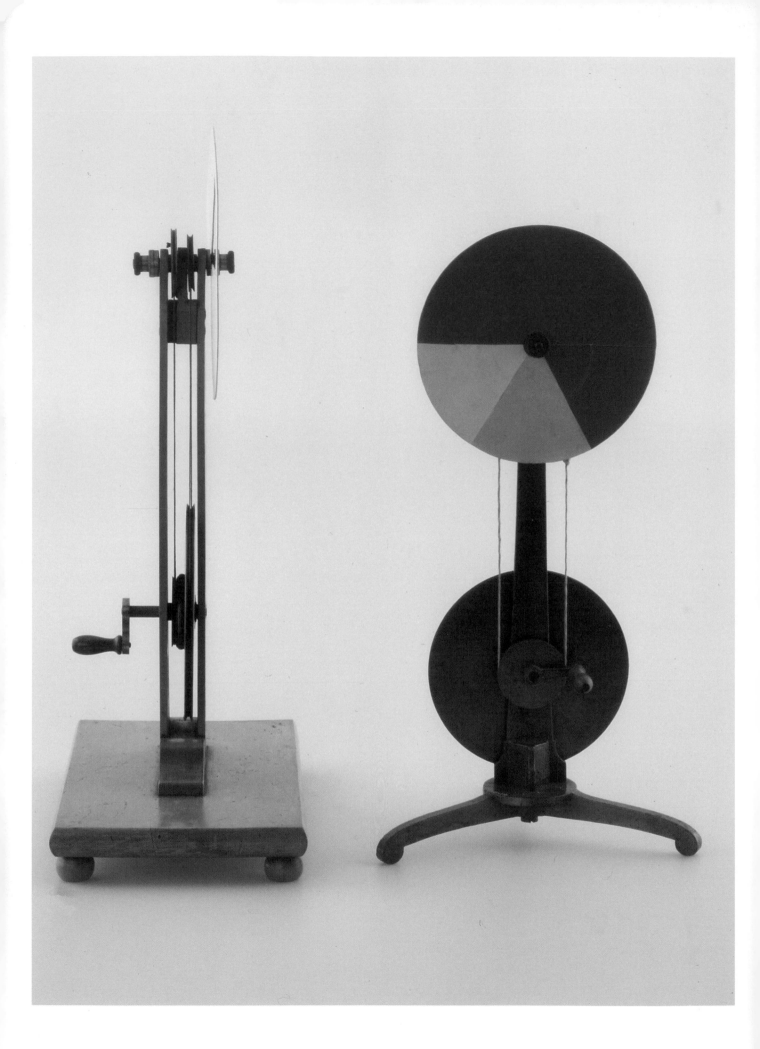

ARTS ET METIERS GRAPHIQUES

LETTRES

18 RUE SEGUIER PARIS 6

FREGIO MECANO

(Carattere scomponibile)

Minimo Kg. 2,50

Si vendono anche figure separate: minimo Kg. 1 per figura

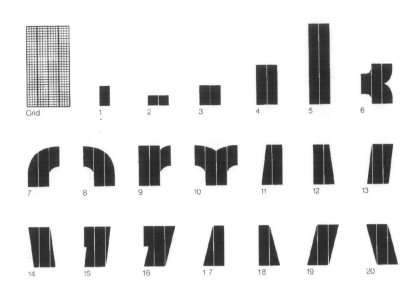

Grid   1   2   3   4   5   6

7   8   9   10   11   12   13

14   15   16   17   18   19   20

abcdefghijk

lmnopqrſstu

unxyz

This type is set with typographical material (Brass Rule) The letter ca: below shows how the individual pieces are assembled.

aaaaaaß

graphische abteilung der

nürttembergischen

staatlichen

A specimen showing the possibilities in letter formation

kunstgenerbeschule stuttgart

School of decorative Art, Stuttgart. Brass Rule Letters

CONSTRUCTED LETTERS

AA B CC DD
EE FF G HH
I J K LL M
NN O PP Q
RR SS TT UU
V W X Y Z
Æ Œ Ç & Cie
( ) . , ; : ' - « » ! ?
1 2 3 4 5 6 7 8 9 0

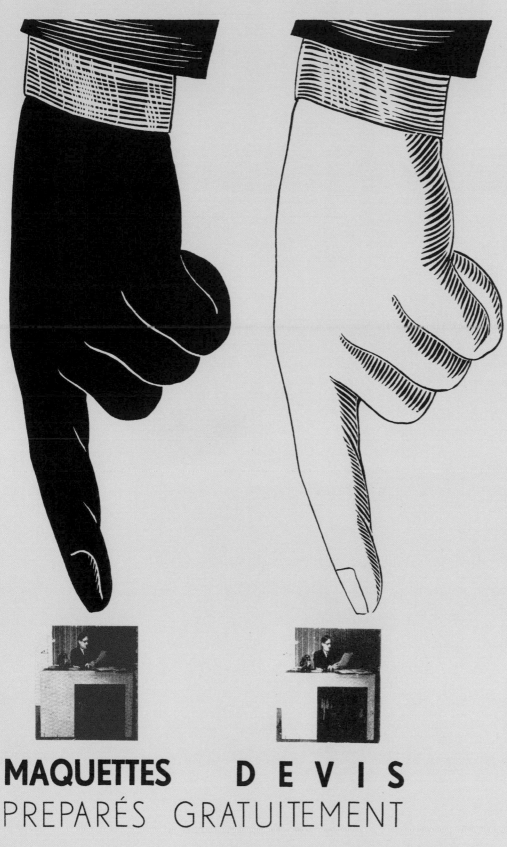

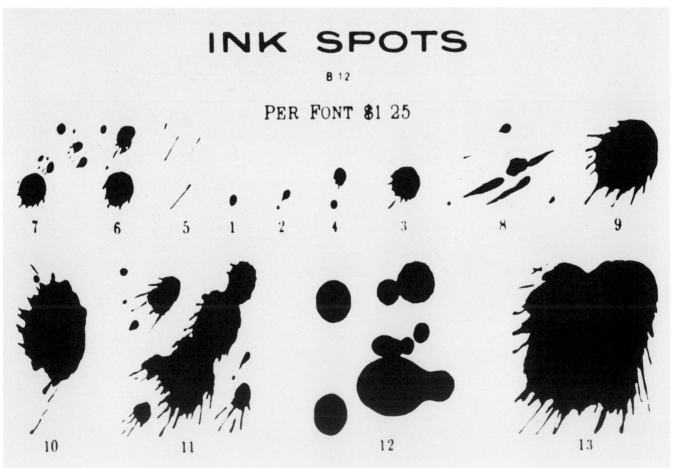

INK SPOTS

B 12

PER FONT $1 25

abcdefghij

klmnopqrs

tuvwxyz

1234567890

TELEFON ČÍS.
2 6 1 7

AᴿCHITEKT PᴀVLOVSKÝ
BRATISLAVA

projektuje a provádí
veškeré stavby
hospodářské
a městské

STAVITEL
ARCHITEKT
F. PAVLOVSKÝ, BRATISLAVA

K. BRANIŠ

K. BRANIŠ

DOPISNICE

casco

fried a spol. - kom. společnost - praha II, vodičkova ulice 20 - telefon 361-93

f·pavlovský

stavitel
architekt
bratislava

KAREL BRANIŠ | dovoluji si oznámiti, že
S CHOTÍ VĚROU | slavili občanský sňatek
 | dne 20. prosince 1930
ROZ. VAŇKOVOU | o 10. hodině dopolední
 | v Brandýse nad Labem

Mojmír Urbánek | PRAHA II · MOZARTEUM

HUDEBNINY · GRAMOFONY

naše značka | vaše značka | váš dopis | praha, dne

Přeložením chráněn obrázek-Fussmotell. | J. TESAŘ

KOUMAR
OBLÉKNE VÁS ELEGANTNĚ
PRAHA II
VE SMEČKÁCH ČÍSLO 27

J. ŠERAN

a·Heger PRAHA XII, TŘÍDA MARŠÁLA FOCHE 6

UMĚLECKOPRŮMYSLOVÉ ZÁVODY

PRAHA-VINOHRADY, DNE | 193

L. KRÁL

životy i auta chrání

NÁRAZNÍK CASCO

FRIED A SPOL.
PRAHA II.
VODIČKOVA 20

P. ŠONDA

MOJMÍR URBÁNEK

HUDEBNINY

PRAHA II, MOZARTEUM

LUXOR-GARAGE, PRAHA
KARLÍN, VÍTKOVA ULICE 18 - TELEFON 3437

ARTS ET MÉTIERS GRAPHIQUES

A B C D E F
G H I J K L M
N O P Q R S T
U V W X Y Z

a b c d e f g h i
j k l m n o p q r s
t u v w x ij y z
1 2 3 4 5 6 7 8 9 0

ĀBCDEFGHI
JKLMNŌPQ
RSTŪVWXY
Z I 2 3 4
5 6 7 8 9 0

144

HNBDIČRMKÉ
GOPAVSYUWL
JSTZXFMYJQ!,
1234567890:
abrphxfcvdń,
stgmjuyeikz

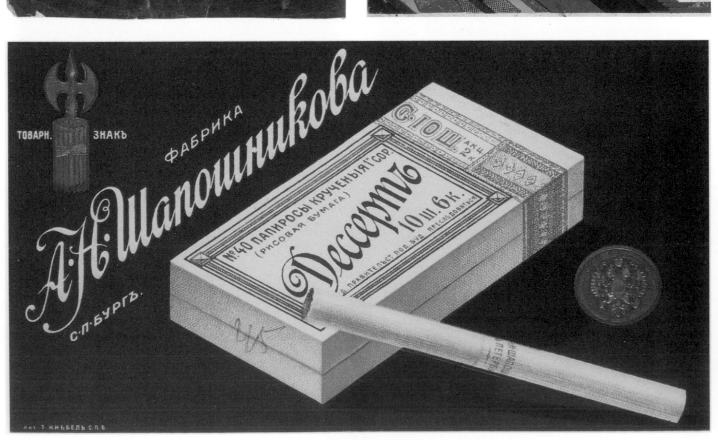

КЛАСИЦИСТИЧНА АНТИКВА

А Б В Г Д Е

Ж З И Й К Л М

Н О П Р С Т У

Ф Х Ц Ч Ш Щ

Ъ Ь Ю Я

1 2 3 4 5 6 7 8 9 0

A B C D E
F G H I J
K L M N O
P Q R S T
U V X Y Z

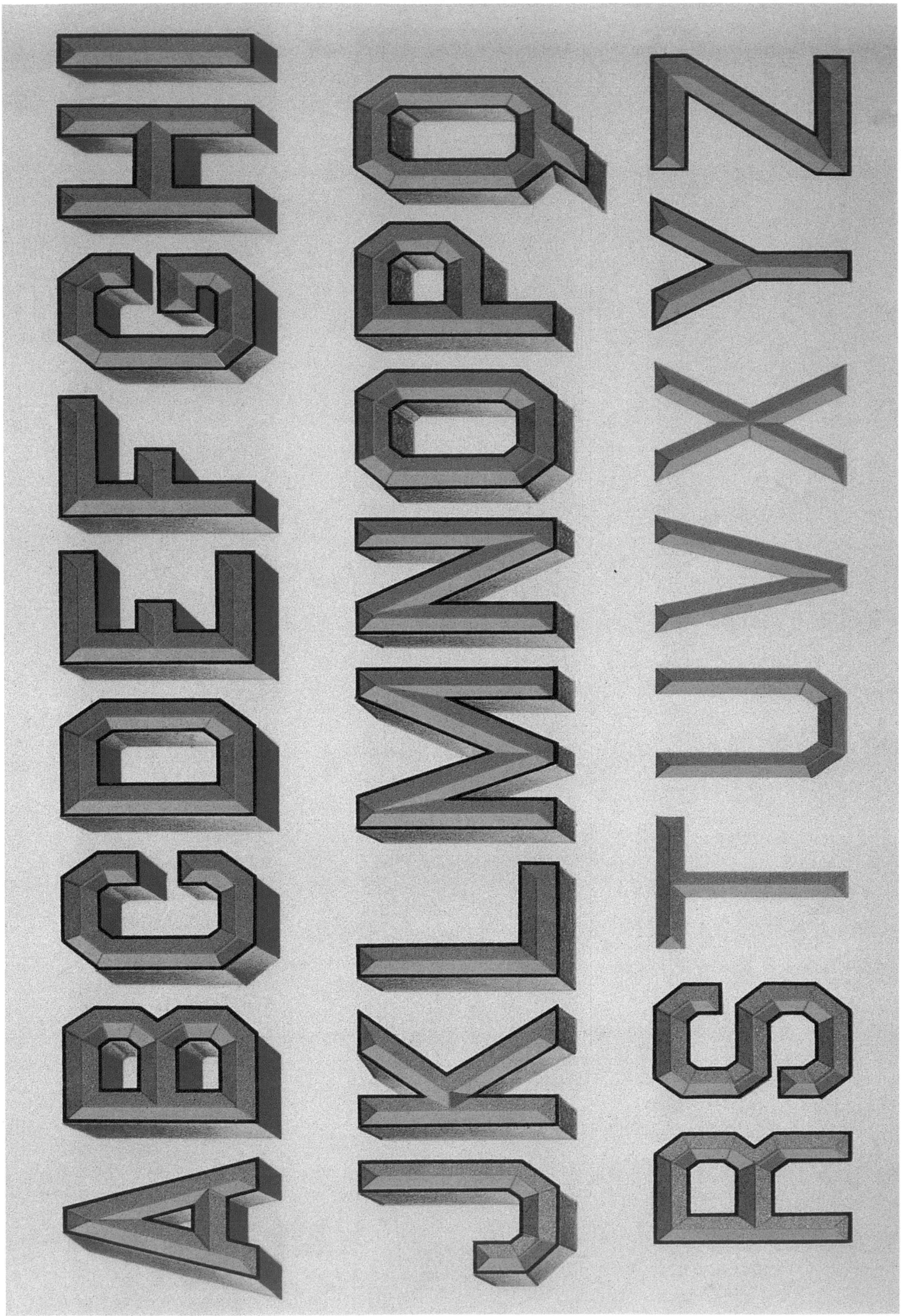
ABCDEFGHI
JKLMNOPQ
RSTUVXYZ

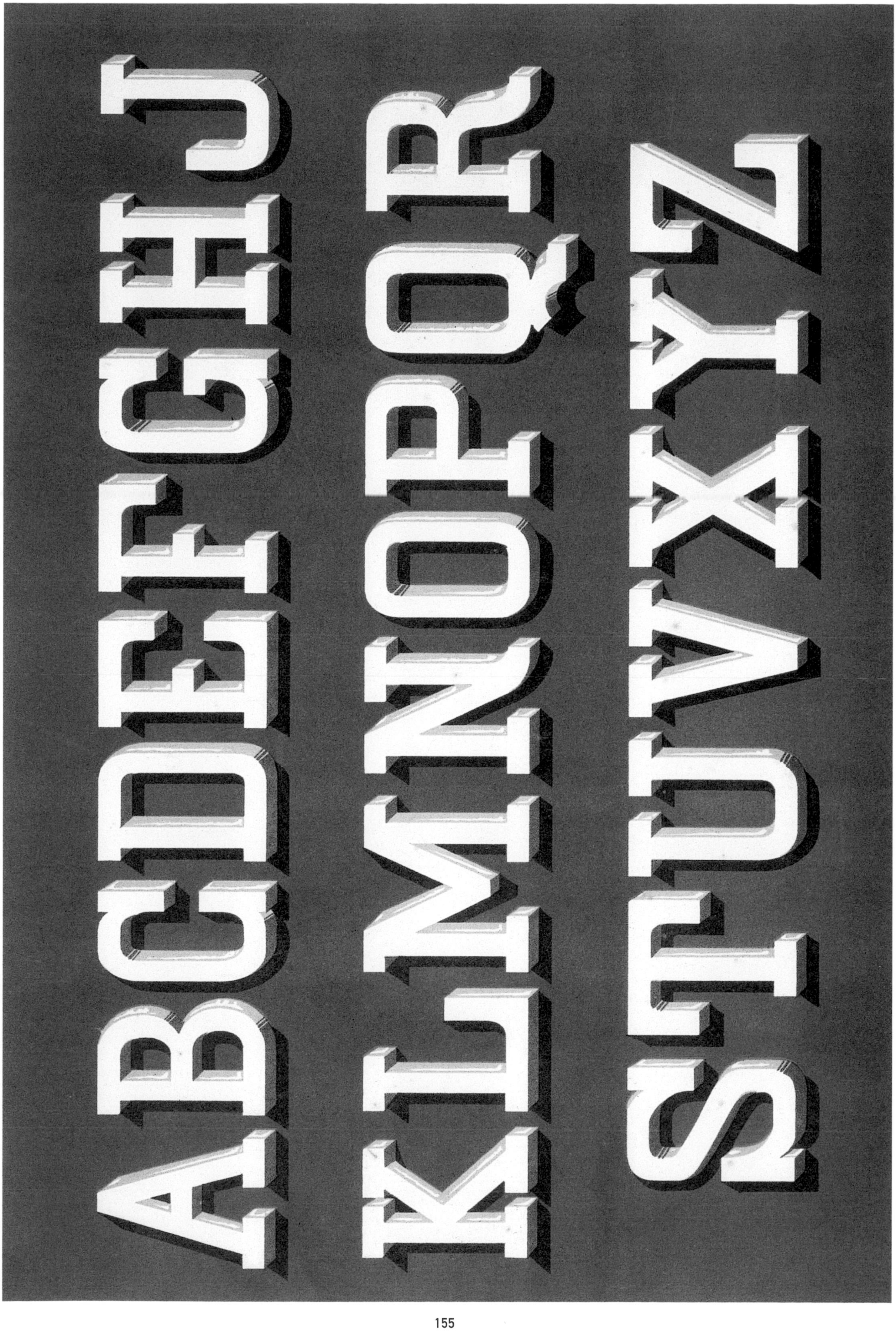
ABCDEFGHJ
KLMNOPQR
STUVXYZ

ABCDEFGHIJ
KLMNOPQRS
TUVXYZ

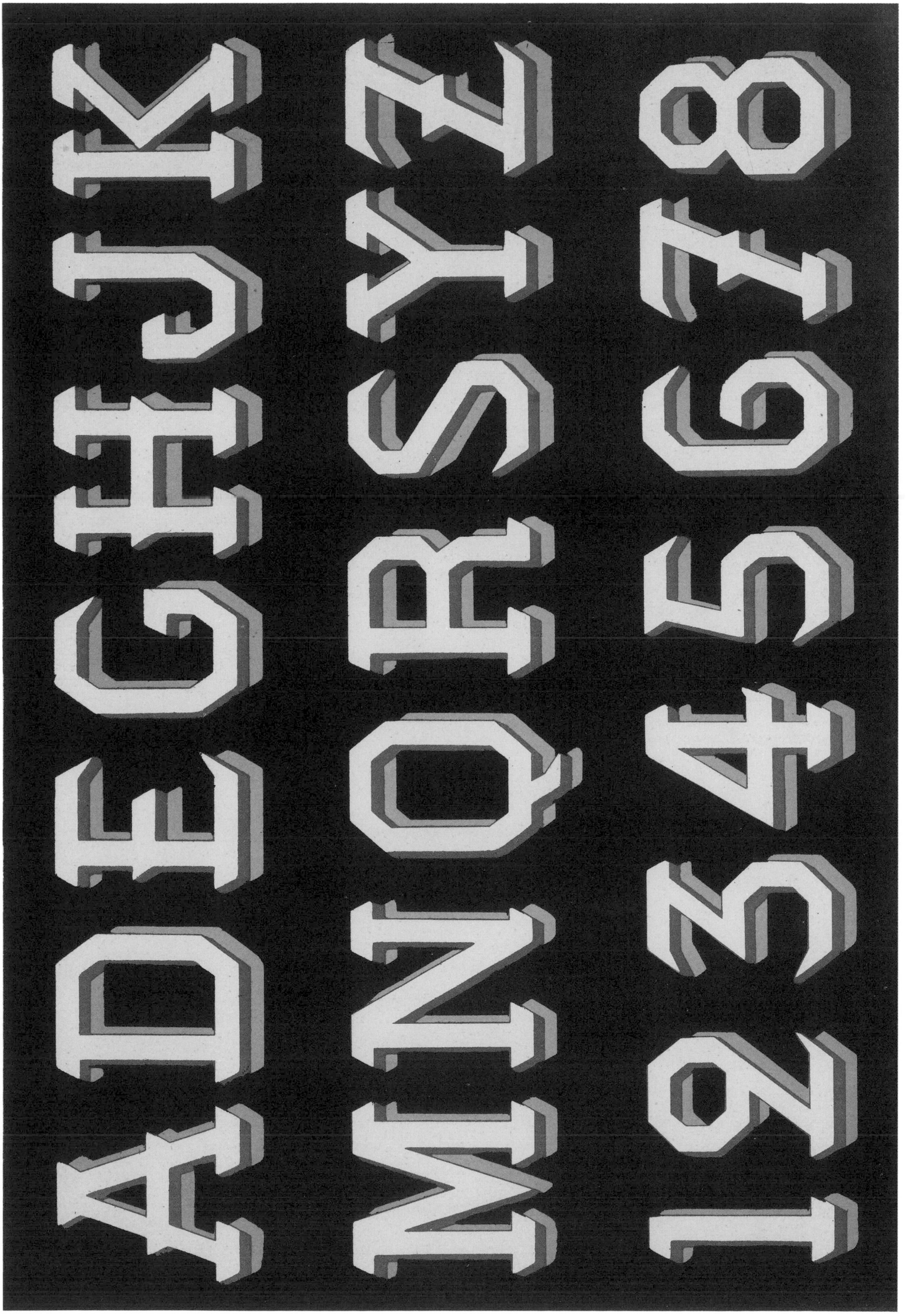
ADEGHJK
MNQRSYZ
12345678

·abcdefghij
klmnopqr
stuvwxyz

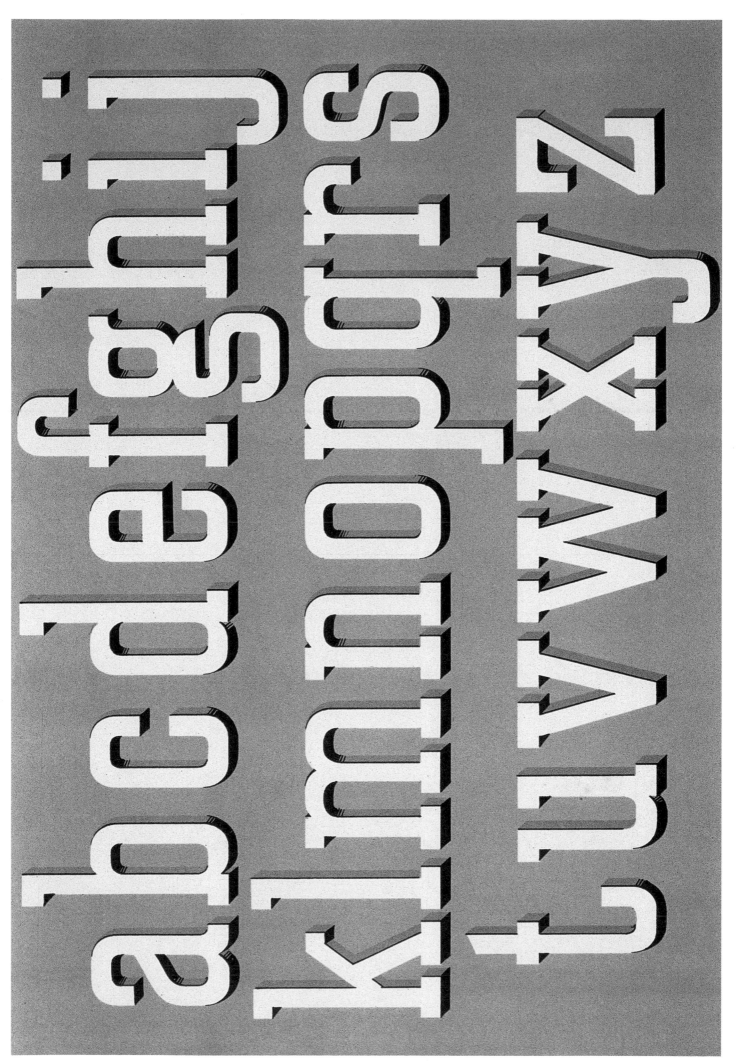

abcdef
ghijklm
nopqrs
tuvxyz
1234567890.&

O 74

164

COMPAGNONS DE COCAGNE

MENU POTAGE VELOUTÉ CAROLINE • ENDIVES AU JUS
DU 12 NOVEMBRE
CHEZ
VINCENT
CANDRÉ
RUE SAINT
ANDRÉ
DES ARCS

TURBOT DE DIEPPE AU BEURRE D'ISIGNY • PERDREAUX FLANQUÉS D'ALOUETTES

VIN ROSÉ DE BOLÈNE
VIN BLANC DE POUILLY-SUR-LOIRE
PINOT DU SANCERROIS
CHAVIGNOLE
CAFÉ
FINE ET ARMAGNAC

COQ A LA BERRICHONNE

HARICOTS VERTS
SALADE PANACHÉE
FROMAGES

POMMES BONNE FEMME

CORBEILLE DE FRUITS

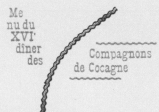

Menu du XVIᵉ dîner des Compagnons de Cocagne

MARMITE M
NORMANDE. TURBAN A
D'ANGUILLE AU CHA-
BLIS. SELLE DE VEAU FAR-
CIE ORLOFF AVEC UNE GAR-
NITURE PRINTANIÈRE. ASPER-
GES DE VINEUIL SAUCE HOL-
LANDAISE. CŒUR DE ROMAI-
NE A L'HUILE D'OLIVE. FRO-
MAGES. FRAISES CHAN-
TILLY. CORBEILLE
DE FRUITS. CAFÉ.

CON
BLANC
EN CA-
RAFE.
FLEUR
IE EN PI-
CHET.
GEVREY
CHAM-
BERTIN
EAUX-
DE-VIE DU PAYS

ABCDEFG
HIJKLMN
OPQRSTU
VWXYZ&!

abcdefghijklmn

opqrstuvwxyz!

123456789

ABCDEFGHIJKLMNOPQR
STUVWXYZ★12345 6789★?

abcdefghijklm
nopqrstuvwxyz

VARIETY
·
VARIETY

−it's the RESULT that COUNTS !

ABCDEFGHIJKL
MNOPQRSTUVWX
YZ123456789?

VARIETY

ABCDEFGHIJKL
MNOPQRSTUVW
XYZ123456789

VARIETY

Ever Ready LABELS GO PLACES and DO THINGS

528 IDEAS for AMERICAN BUSINESS

Save Time   Save Money   Speed Production

169

AAAAAAAABB
CCCDDEEEFF
GGHHIJJKKK
LLLMMMMMNN
NNOOPPPQRRS
STTUUUUUVVV
IJWWWXXYYZ&
1234567890 10
(.,:„"!§?';-)

ČTYŘCICERO „PATRONA" GROTESK RUSKÉ

А Б В Г Д Е Ж З И I
А БВ ВV ГG ДD Е ЖŽ ЗZ ИN I

Й К Л М Н О П Р С
ЙJ К ЛL М НN О ПР РR СS

Т У Ф Х Ц Ч Ш Щ Ъ
Т УU ФF ХCH ЦС ЧČ ШŠ ЩŠČ Ъ

Ы Ь Ѣ Э Ю Я Ѳ Ѵ
ЫU Ь ѢĚ ЭE ЮJU ЯJA ѲF ѴI neb V

Љ Њ Ћ Ђ Ј Џ Ж Ӝ
ЉLJ ЊŇ ЋТ ЂĎ ЈJ ЏDŽ ЖА ЊJA

В. А. ФРАНЦЕВЪ
ПРАГА

171

ARAGÓN

ABCDEFGHI

JKLMNÑOPQ

ASTUVWXYZ

Æ .,;: Œ

abcdefghikl
moprstuvw
xyz

A B C
D E F G H
I J K L M
N O P Q R
S T U V W
X Y Z

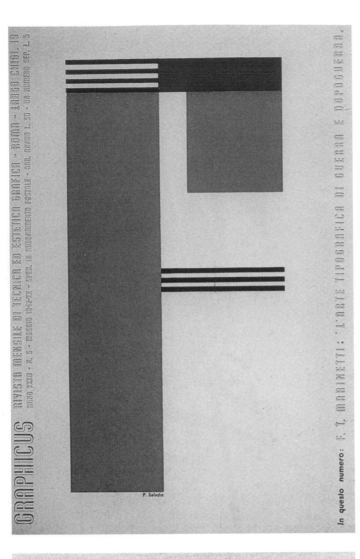

GRAPHICUS RIVISTA MENSILE DI TECNICA ED ESTETICA GRAFICA · ROMA · LARGO CHIGI, 19 ANNO XXXII · N. 5 · GENNAIO 1947-XX · SPED. IN ABBONAMENTO POSTALE · ABB. ANNUO SEP. L. 5 · UN NUMERO SEP. L. 5

In questo numero: F. T. MARINETTI: "L'ARTE TIPOGRAFICA DI GUERRA E DOPOGUERRA.

P. Saladin

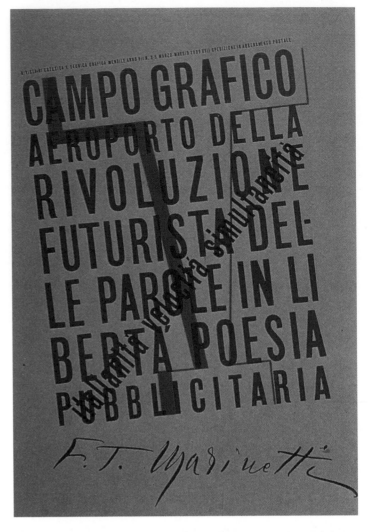

RIVISTA DI ESTETICA E TECNICA GRAFICA MENSILE ANNO VIII N. 3 A MARZO MARZIO 2005 XVII SPEDIZIONE IN ABBONAMENTO POSTALE

CAMPO GRAFICO
AEROPORTO DELLA RIVOLUZIONE FUTURISTA DEL- LE PAROLE IN LI BERTÀ POESIA PUBBLICITARIA

l'aulart'icolsrà simultaneità

F. T. Marinetti

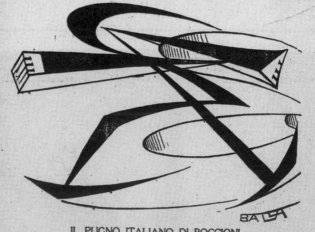

ANNO I. N. 6ª · FIRENZE, 19 AGOSTO 1916 · Esce il 10 e il 25 d'ogni mese · Redazione e Amministrazione Via Brunelleschi 2, FIRENZE · Abbon. Anno L. 2,50 · In numero Cent. 10

L'ITALIA FUTURISTA

DIREZIONE ARTISTICA
BRUNO CORRA · E. SETTIMELLI

E morto UMBERTO BOCCIONI caro grande forte migliore divino genio futurista ieri denigrato oggi glorificato superarlo superarlo superarlo durezza eroismo velocità avanti giovani futuristi tutto tutto doloresanguevita per la grande Italia sgombra ingigantita agilissima elettrica esplosiva non lagrime acciaio acciaio!

MARINETTI

IL PUGNO ITALIANO DI BOCCIONI

Ecco perchè volevano la guerra, egli e i suoi amici, quando nessuno la pensava, perchè sapevano quanto ingiusta fosse la svalutazione delle forze nazionali e quante oscure potenti radici avrebbero germogliato il giorno che la coscienza delle proprie forze le avesse nutrite.

A Parigi, a Monaco, a Berlino, ovunque si parlasse male dell'Italia fuori d'Italia, Boccioni con la sua violenza e col suo ingegno si batteva coraggiosamente.

ABCDEFGHIJ
KLMNOPQRS
TUVWXYZ$!?
1234567890

ABCDEFGHIJKL
MNOPQRSTUV
WXYZ&.,-':;!?
$1234567890

EL

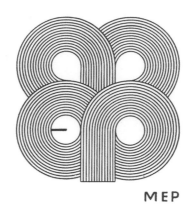

MEP

MA

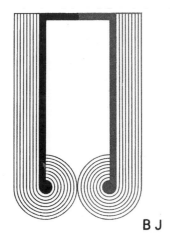

BJ

DT

SJ

MODÈLES DE

JEAN PUIFORCAT

SE

BC

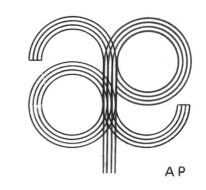

AP

KONSTRUKTIVISMUS
IN THEORIE UND PRAXIS

Ein Gespräch ● Sprecher **A** ein erster Akzidenzer, **B** ein Bachulke ● Kollege **B** spinnt: Na, da habt'r ja wieder was Schönes eingerührt! **A** Ach, Sie meinen wohl die „elementare typographie"? **B** Nu freilich, man spricht doch heute nur noch von der „neuen Kunst"—?—Da muss ich gleich lachen! Der alte Gutenberg wird sich im Grabe rumdrehen über solche Kunst! **A** Haben Sie denn nicht seinerzeit in dem TM-Heft gelesen, dass die Konstruktivisten den Krieg an alle „Kunst" erklärt haben? **B** Nee, was da alles geschrieben wurde, ist mir viel zu hoch. Das kann so'n simpler alter Knabe wie ich nicht mehr verdauen. Aber ihr Jungen, ihr seid ja helle! **A** Ich muss auch sagen, dass die Häufung von gleichbedeutenden Fremdwörtern das Verständnis der Sache nur erschwert, und es wäre besser gewesen, die Artikel mehr für den Laien gedacht zu schreiben. **B** Ja, sie müssten „elementarer" sein! **A** Nun aber die Beispiele, was meinen Sie dazu? **B** So'ne Frage! Lächerlich, verrückt natürlich. Wenn sich das früher einer gewagt hätte, wäre er zum Tempel raus geflogen. **A** Das haben Sie bisher immer gesagt, wenn etwas Neues kam, und dann hat man sich daran gewöhnt, ja selber mitgemacht. **B** Davon kann hier keine Rede sein. Das geht jedem Buchdrucker von Fleisch und Blut gegen den Strich. Gequirlter Satz und Fischhaufen gehören abgelegt, aber nicht gedruckt! **A** Ach, das bezieht sich wohl auf Seite 196 und 201 des TM-Heftes? Ja, es gibt eben bei jeder Sache Übergriffe, und dann ist ja das ganze Thema Konstruktivismus erst ein Weg, noch kein Ziel. **B** Besser gesagt, es ist alles noch

BRIEFKOPF-ENTWURF

SIGNET DER ORTSGRUPPE DRESDEN
ENTWURF WALTHER KÖNIG DRESDEN

unreif. Na, das sieht man ja auch! **A** Sie dürfen das nicht so verallgemeinern, lieber Kollege. Entschieden sind Beispiele zu sehen, denen man ihre Berechtigung nicht absprechen kann, die in ihrer betonten Einfachheit und Sachlichkeit eine gute Wirkung haben. **B** Und die Kolumnenziffer, he? Ist das auch Einfachheit, Sachlichkeit, wenn man sie erst suchen muss? **A** Die Konstruktivisten sind bestrebt, alles anders zu machen, wie bisher. Und

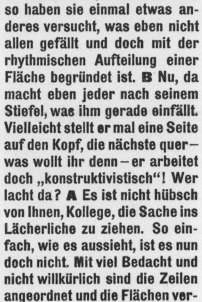

so haben sie einmal etwas anderes versucht, was eben nicht allen gefällt und doch mit der rhythmischen Aufteilung einer Fläche begründet ist. **B** Nu, da macht eben jeder nach seinem Stiefel, was ihm gerade einfällt. Vielleicht stellt er mal eine Seite auf den Kopf, die nächste quer— was wollt ihr denn—er arbeitet doch „konstruktivistisch"! Wer lacht da? **A** Es ist nicht hübsch von Ihnen, Kollege, die Sache ins Lächerliche zu ziehen. So einfach, wie es aussieht, ist es nun doch nicht. Mit viel Bedacht und nicht willkürlich sind die Zeilen angeordnet und die Flächen verteilt. Machen Sie doch den Versuch und füllen Sie eine weisse Fläche mit verschieden gearteten und geformten Elementen, die Sie sich vielleicht aus schwarzem Papier schneiden, und Sie werden die Schwierigkeit erkennen, die sich ergibt, wenn man etwas organisch gestalten will. **B** Was hat denn diese Spielerei mit uns zu tun? Wir machen das, was man uns sagt, und haben uns im übrigen den Wünschen und Angaben der Kunden zu fügen, und die werden sich für solche tote Klötzer-Manier bestens bedanken. **A** Einfachheit kann man nicht als tot bezeichnen, und ich versichere Ihnen, dass es

ALEXANDER MATHEJA DRESDEN

Betracht, und so wird auch für die elementare Typographie meist die Groteskschrift verwendet, weil sie das Ursprüngliche in der Schrift am meisten verkörpert und ohne persönliche Merkmale ist. Hier bei dieser Karte aber wurde die Neuland-Type verwendet, ohne störend zu wirken. Mit solchen Experimenten heisst es aber vorsichtig sein. **B** Was soll denn nun aus den vielen anderen schönen Schriften werden, wenn wirklich die neue Kunst um sich greift? **A** Bisher haben die Groteskschriften ungestört in der Ecke gelegen, und nun werden sie eben mal dran kommen. Ist das nicht ein gerechter Ausgleich? **B** Ach, darum ist wohl der Text der Beilage auch gleich so gesetzt, ich meine in Grotesk. Vielleicht gar aus Sympathie?— **A** 0, Sie alter Zyniker! Hier kam es doch auf eine ruhige, möglichst kräftige Type an, welche die Beispiele gut hervortreten lässt. **B** Na, klotzig genug sieht sie auch aus. **A** Aber gut in der Flächenwirkung. Wie gefällt Ihnen denn die Aufmachung dieser Beilage in der neuen Art? Jedenfalls ein Mittelweg, der auch für Prospekte usw. gut geeignet wäre. **B** Nun ja, aber ich weiss nicht, hübsch ist anders. **A** Ich finde gerade, dass sich die Seiten mit den Ecken ganz gut ausnehmen. Es liegt Abwechslung darin. **B** Ja, im Fahrten- und Abenteuerbuch liegt auch Abwechslung, ein Bild so und eins so. Ich kann nicht sagen, dass das „sachlich" ist. **A** Freilich hatte auch ich mir gedacht, dass Tschichold andere Wege der Buchkunst finden würde. Vielleicht hat er sich bewusst bezähmt; vielleicht hat auch die Büchergilde ein Wort mitgesprochen. **B** Die werden sowieso am Umsatz der Bücher den „Erfolg" (?) merken! **A** Sie meinen wohl, dass durch die neue Ausstattung die Zahl der Mitglieder steigt? **B** Das wollen wir erst mal sehen! **A** Nun hören Sie mal. Falls Sie auch Lust haben sollten, sich mal in Konstruktivismus zu versuchen, will ich Ihnen ein paar Thesen mit auf den Weg geben: I. Typographie kann unter Umständen Kunst sein. II. Gestaltung ist Wesen aller Kunst, die typographische Gestaltung ist nicht Abmalen des textlichen Inhalts. III. Auch die nichtbedruckten Stellen sind positive Werte. IV. Qualität der Type bedeutet Einfachheit und Schönheit. Die Einfachheit schliesst in sich Klarheit, eindeutige, zweckentsprechende Form, Verzicht auf allen entbehrlichen Ballast. Schönheit bedeutet gutes Ausbalancieren der Fläche. Die Forderung an die Typographie ist — **B** Hören Sie auf, mir wird ganz schlecht! **A** Schön! Für heute wollen wir dieses Thema abbrechen, beherzigen Sie meine Worte und verwerten Sie das Gute des „Elementaren". **B** Eigentlich war es überhaupt Unfug, sich darüber noch lange zu unterhalten und vier Seiten kostbares Papier zu vergeuden, denn wir stehen ja heute mitten im Konstruktivismus, und es wird nicht lange dauern, bis auch diese Sensation ihr Ende gefunden hat. Denn so war's und ist's noch in der Welt: Im steten Wechsel liegt ja der Reiz des Lebens. **A** Ei, Donnerwetter, Sie sprechen ja so geistreich und verständig! — Gewiss vereinbart sich nicht alles im Konstruktivismus mit unseren bisherigen Anschauungen über Typographie, aber die für ihn erbrachten Begründungen sind nicht ohne weiteres von der Hand zu weisen. Der grösste Teil seiner Widersacher stützt sich meistens auf unbestimmte Gefühle. Wollen wir doch froh sein, dass wir aus der „elementaren typographie" neue Anregungen und Gedanken gewonnen haben, die leider oft in ganz falscher Verkennung der inneren Zusammenhänge weidlich ausgenutzt werden und so bei dem kritischen Beschauer ein nicht immer befriedigendes Gefühl auslösen. **B** Jedenfalls hat man um die neue Art Satzgruppierung, die man plötzlich mit „Kunst" bezeichnet, viel zuviel Wesens gemacht. Drum sei auch der Debatte ein Punkt gesetzt.

BERATUNGEN
UND ENTWÜRFE
WERBEDRUCKE

GEORG KLEMM
NICOLAISTR. 22
FERNRUF 35308

T
REKLAME
DRESDEN~A.16

GESCHÄFTSKARTE ENTWURF HANS MENKE DRESDEN

Wij garandeeren
bij afkoeling na verwarming
van den kabel een

Vlakke
karakteristiek

en **tóch**

een soepelen kabel

20

ELECTRICITEIT BOUWT STEDEN

Aenne Biermann

60 **Fotos**	mit Einleitung von Franz Roh	»Der literarische Foto-Streit«
60 **photos**	with introduction by Franz Roh	"The literary dispute about photography"
60 **photographies**	avec introduction par Franz Roh	«La querelle au sujet de la photographie»

Fototek 2   Klinkhardt & Biermann   Verlag - Publishers - Editeurs   Berlin W 10

L. Moholy-Nagy

60 Fotos
60 photos
60 photographies

Fototek 1   Klinkhardt & Biermann   Verlag - Publishers - Editeurs   Berlin W 10

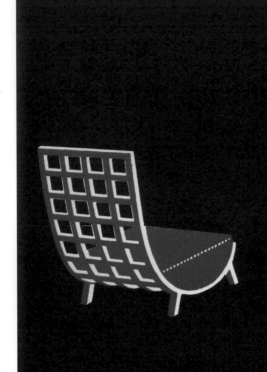

EINZELMÖBEL
UND NEUZEITLICHE
RAUMKUNST

HERAUSGEGEBEN
VON ALEXANDER
KOCH DARMSTADT

TYPOGRAPHICAL SIGNETS

School of decorative Art, Stuttgart, Professor Veit. Signets
composed of brass rules and typographical borders.

FORUM maandblad voor architectuur en gebonden kunsten

12/1953

KESTNER-GESELLSCHAFT
E.V. HANNOVER
KÖNIGSTRASSE 8

WINTER

PROGRAMM

1928-1929

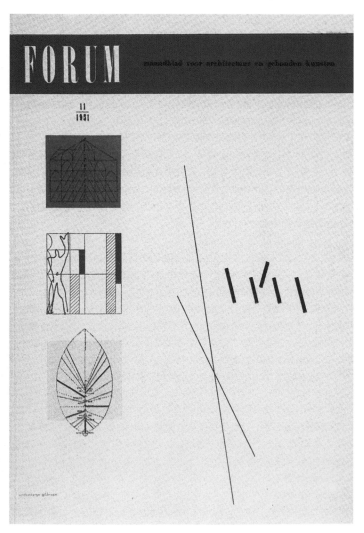

FORUM maandblad voor architectuur en gebonden kunsten

11/1951

DER VORBILDLICHE WERBEDRUCK

А Б В Г Д Е

Ж З И К Л М

Н О П Р С Т

У Ф Х Ц Ч Щ

Ъ Ы Э Ю Я

Таб. I. К Проблеме Композиции:

И. Клюн 1942 г.

The art of lay-out nowadays owes its strength to its free use of processes. From photographic apparatus, scissors, a bottle of Indian ink, a gum-pot, combined with the hand of the designer and an un-prejudiced eye, a composition can be evolved and a novel idea expressed by simple means.

SILENCE

THE ART OF LAYOUT

Mise en Page: The Theory and Practice of Layout, by A. Tolmer, was published by *The Studio* magazine in 1932. The genius of the booklet was to instruct by example, and its texts were models of modernist economy and grace. The virtues it sought to inculcate were those of simplicity, balance, clarity of expression, and freedom from preconceptions on the use of materials and processes. Apart from its exemplary value as a design manual what gives *Mise en Page* an undeniable poignancy is the conviction it professes, in text and design, in the necessity to civilized life of principled thought and humane feeling in good practice. For Tolmer, as for Wittgenstein, it seems, "ethics and aesthetic are one."

P R E F A C E

ike skating or walking the tight-rope, the art of lay-out is an art of balance.

t cannot however be expressed merely as a mathematical calculation. The tight-rope walker steadies herself with her parasol rather than with the aid of a formula. The sense of stability; the right and the wrong way of doing anything; the amount of air that enables the earth to breathe; the amount of sleep that permits of the greatest activity during the day; the most satisfactory way of combining the elements of a theatre-set, the page of a book or a poster; all these things are essentially a matter of feeling.

he feelings of mankind are unaffected by the change of ideas, constructive and destructive by turns, which accompany each phase of history. Since the earliest times known to us, love, hate, joy, suffering and religion have exercised a constant influence. Every age and every civilization, therefore, must be guided by these basic impulses and the works produced under their influence, in order to test, control, and correct its own balance.

So, considering the past, we might have written simply an historical study of the kind of balance represented by the art of lay-out. But this we have wished to avoid. If an historical evolution may be traced in the series of illustrations here reproduced it will not be by any means complete.

An investigation has been made into the origins of the art of lay-out. The part played by the shape of text in a lay-out has been demonstrated by reference to various types of ancient writing. The links between letterpress, ornament, and architecture have been pointed out. Points of comparison between modes of lay-out used in different countries and at different periods have been established. The sole aim, however, has been that of providing rich materials for the modern method of approach.

It is always a difficult matter for the professional tennis-player to discuss his game. But this is not a series of lessons in lay-out. We wish to immerse our readers in the subject and to prime them with information which will enable them to infuse fresh life and a continually changing novelty into their practice of it.

There is no technique of which modern publicity has not made use. Arrangements of cut-outs and cut paper have given a new direction to photographic advertising. We shall soon be seeing three-dimensional posters on the hoadings.

ABOM

Photography gives concrete form to the subtlest thoughts. It has the gift of imparting to the dullest, most mechanical and impersonal things the sensitiveness and poetry which admits them into our dreams.

Е. ПАВЛОВ

ВАЛЬС ПАМЯТИ СКРЯБИНА

для фортепиано

E. PAWLOW.

valse

A LA mémoire de *Scriàbine.*

Государственное Музыкальное Издательство.

МОСКВА 1922.

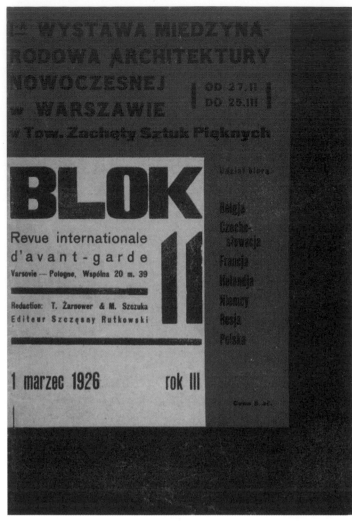

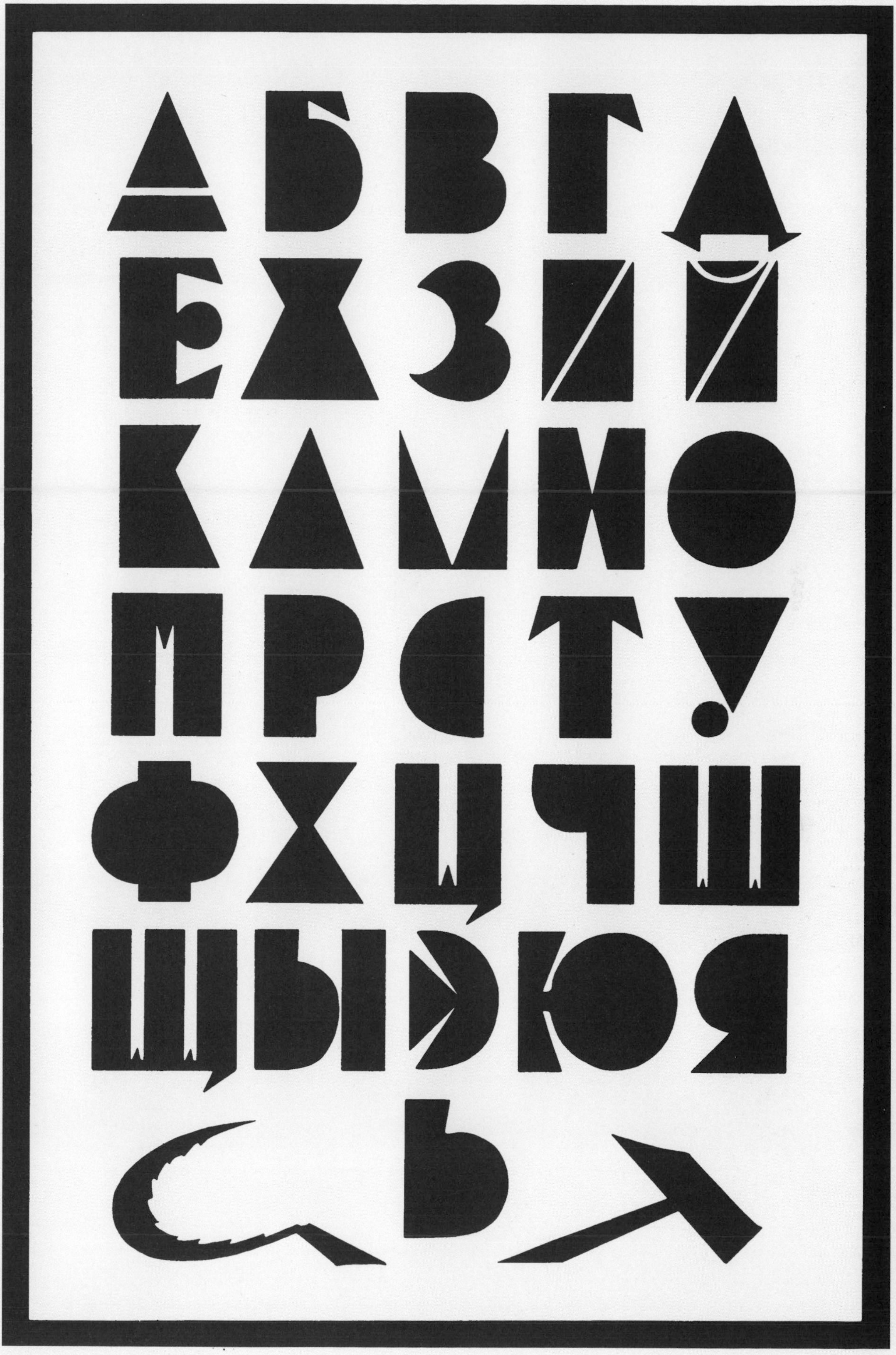
АБВГД
ЕЖЗИЙ
КЛМНО
ПРСТУ
ФХЦЧШ
ЩЫЭЮЯ
Ь

TESA

VETROFLEX

+GF+

LABEL

SOCIETEIT voor CULTUREELE SAMENWERKING

EXCELSIOR THEATER
ZEESTRAAT

GASTVOORSTELLINGEN
DIE JUNGE TRUPPE
(BERLIN)

18 TOT 23 JANUARI 1931
DER ANDERE
VON MIGUEL DE UNAMUNO
DEUTSCH von OTTO BUCK
DRAMA IN DREI AKTEN MIT EINEM EPILOG

DER ANDERE . . . . GILLIS van RAPPARD

LAURA . . . . ELLEN DAGMAR

DIAMIANA . . . . SYBIL RARES

ERNESTO. . . . . EMILIO CARGHER

AVITO . . . . HANS ALVA

DIE AMME. . . . . ERIKA KRISTEN

REGIE: GILLIS van RAPPARD

PRIJZEN der PLAATSEN

ZAAL 1e DEEL FL. 3.00 ZAAL 2e DEEL FL. 2.50

ZAAL 3e DEEL en BALCON FL. 1.25

PLAATSEN TE BESPREKEN DAGELIJKS

AAN HET GEBOUW VAN 10 TOT 16 UUR

VAN 24 TOT 31 JANUARI
DIE QUADRATUR DES KREISES
LUSTSPIEL von VAL: KATAJEW

ONTWERP V. HUSZAR

VWMNK

OCSQGA

XYZIEFL

UDBRP

JTH;,!?:

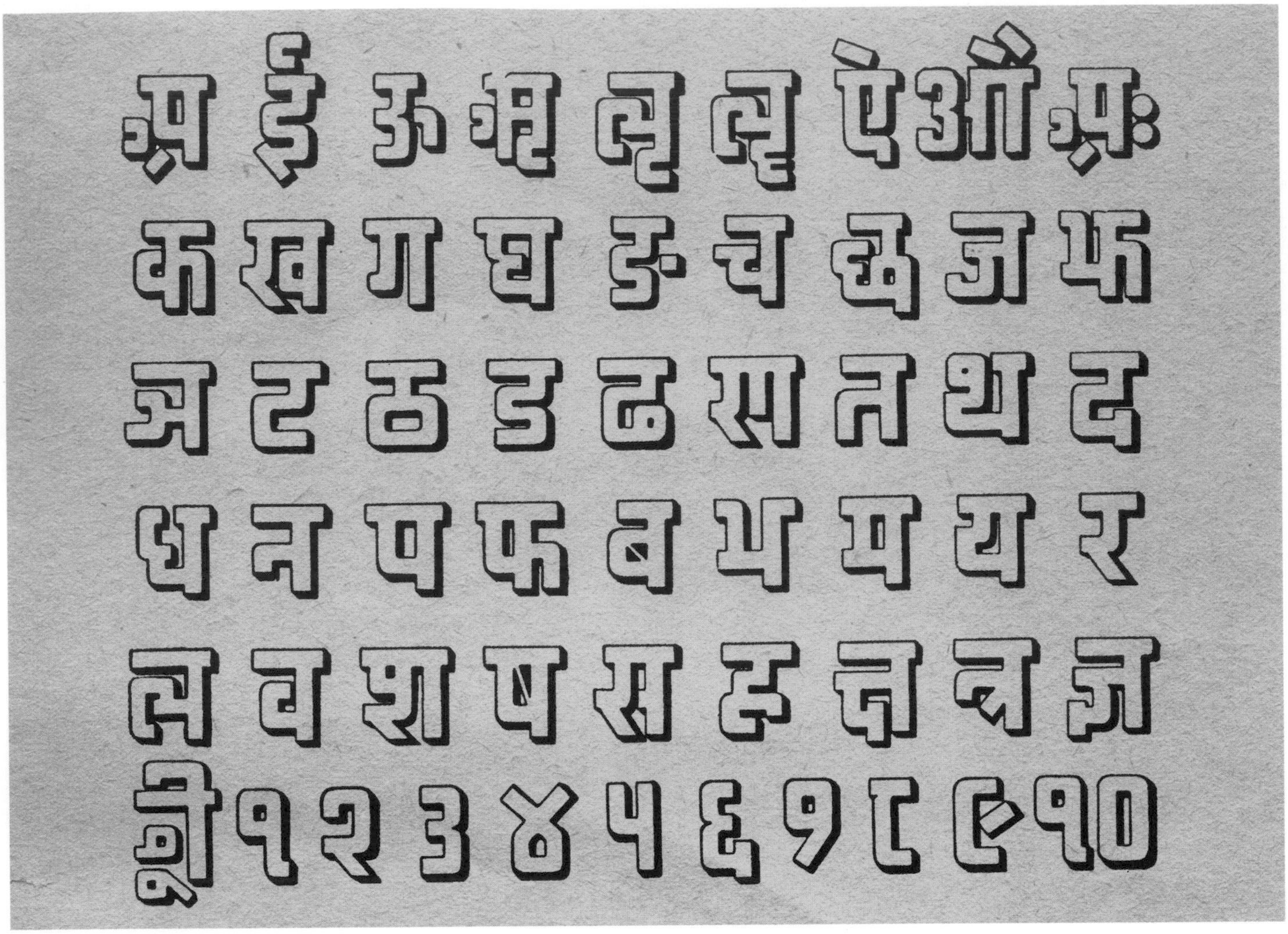
अ ई ऊ ऋ ऌ ॡ ऐ ऑ अः
क ख ग घ ङ च छ ज झ
ञ ट ठ ड ढ ण त थ द
ध न प फ ब भ म य र
ल व श ष स ह ळ क्ष ज्ञ
श्री १ २ ३ ४ ५ ६ ७ ८ ९ १०

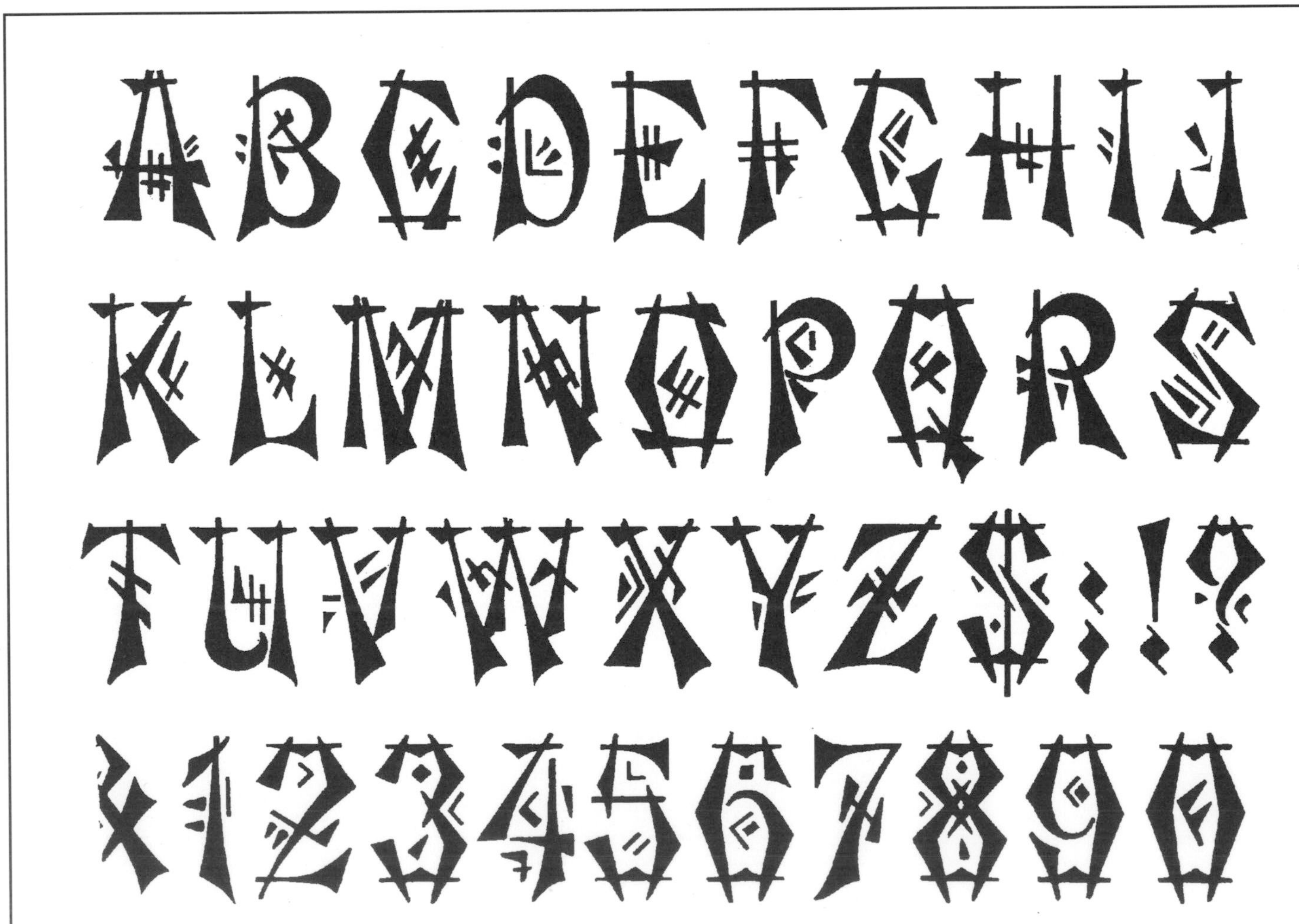
ABCDEFGHIJ
KLMNOPQRS
TUVWXYZ$;!?
&1234567890

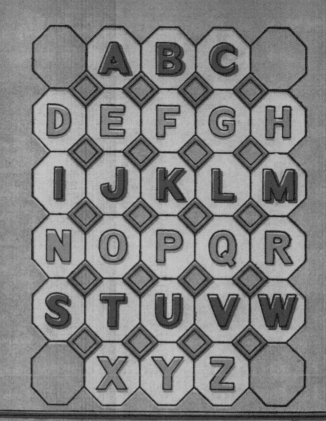

Publishers:
INDIAN BOOK DEPOT
2937, Bahadur Garh Rd.
Delhi-110006

Printers:
INDIAN ART PRESS
A/6, Mayapuri,
New Delhi-110064.

211

Aa Bb Cc Dd Ee Ff Gg

Hh Ii Jj Kk Ll Mm Nn

Oo Pp Qq Rr Ss Tt Uu

Vv Ww Xx Yy Zz

1234567890
1234567890

ABCDE
FGHIJK
LMNOPQ
RSTUV
WXYZ

59   Page from Arts et Métiers Graphiques (Deberny and Peignot, Paris, 1930s). Courtesy David Batterham.

60   Top left: Koishi Kiyoshi, cover for *Shoka-Shinkei (Sensitivity of the early summer)* Japan, 1933. Private collection. Top right: B. Titov, cover for *Nonsense* by V. Woodward, (GIZ, USSR, 1927). Courtesy Misha Anikst. Bottom left: poster for the review *Lacerba*, designer unknown, Italy, 1914. Private collection. Bottom right: cover for *Filmova' Dramata*, screenplays by Louis Delluc (Ladislav Kuncir V Praza Czechoslovakia, 1925). Private collection.

61   Joost Schmidt, Condensed grotesque typeface with construction details and variants of single figures, the Netherlands, 1926. Courtesy Richard Hollis.

62   Printer's advertisement from Gebrauchsgraphik, Germany, 1930s.

63   Top: from a promotional folder for the typeface *Erbar*, Ludwig and Mayer, Germany, 1930s. Courtesy Royal College of Art Library (photograph by Dominic Sweeney). Bottom: from a promotional folder for the printers Gebr. Hartmann, Germany, 1930. Collection Redstone Press.

64   Ladislav Sutnar, covers for books by George Bernard Shaw, Czechoslovakia, early-1930s. Courtesy Museum of Decorative Arts, Prague.

65   Typeface from the *Signwriter's Manual of Typefaces* by Richard Pípal Czechoslovakia, 1956. Collection Redstone Press.

66   Typeface designed for use on buildings by Edward Wright, UK, 1965. Courtesy the Department of Typography and Graphic Communication at The University of Reading.

67   Page from *Hoffmann's Schriftatlas*, (Julius Hoffmann Verlag, Germany, 1930). Private collection.

68   Back cover of *Gebrauchsgraphik*, Germany, 1926. Courtesy Gutenberg Museum, Mainz.

69   Page from *Buffon Alphabet des Oiseaux* (Pellerin and Cie, Paris, 1890). Courtesy Pentagram.

70   Typeface based on Standard Light Extended, Berthold Typefounders, early 20th Century. Private collection.

71   Jan Tschichold, film poster for Abel Gance's *Napoleon*, 1926. Photograph by Dominic Sweeney. Courtesy Royal College of Art Library.

72   Cover of Gebrauchsgraphik, Germany, 1930s, designer unknown. Courtesy The Gutenberg-Museum, Mainz.

73   Logos from an Italian type manufacturer's catalogue, ca 1950. Courtesy David Wakefield.

74   Photomontage by Paul Schuitema, Netherlands, 1928. Courtesy Merrill C. Berman Collection, New York.

75   Typeface from the album *Schriften, Lettering, Ecritures*, 1940s, designer unknown. Courtesy Klingspoor Museum, Germany.

76   Back cover of XXth Century, designer unknown, (English edition Christmas, 1938). Courtesy Brian Webb Collection.

79   Mauricio Amster poster for *Cartilla Escolar Antifascista* (Ministry of Public Information Madrid. 1937), "The Cultural Militias Fight Fascism by Combating Ignorance." Private collection.

80/84   Pages from the *Antifascist Schoolbook*, design and montages by Mauricio Amster, photographs by José val del Omar and José Calandin, Spain, 1937. Courtesy Lutz Becker.

87   Cover for *Sinopsis* by Miguel Prieto, Mexico, 1953. Courtesy Xavier Bermúdez.

88   Miguel Prieto, typography for book covers, poster and newspaper, Mexico, 1950s. Courtesy Xavier Bermúdez.

89   Miguel Prieto, poster for treatment of alcoholism, Mexico ca 1950. Courtesy Xavier Bermúdez.

90   Paul Renner, preliminary drawing for the typeface *Futura*, Germany, 1925. Private collection.

91   Wladyslaw Strzeminski, cover for *Z Ponad* by Julian Przbos, Poland, 1930. Courtesy Merrill C. Berman Collection, New York.

92   A. Kruchenykh, drawing from *Learn Artists*, Russia, 1917. Private collection.

93   Russian block alphabet, designer known, date unknown. Courtesy David Hillman.

94   Alphabet from *Methods of Lettering* by Fridrich Moravcik, Bratislava, 1975. Collection Redstone Press.

95   Top left: cover of *Zlom* by Konstantin Biebel, design by Karel Teige, Czechoslovakia, 1928. © Estate of Karel Teige Private collection. Top right: cover of *Diabolo* by Viteslav Nezval design by H. V. Obrtel, Czechoslovakia, 1926. Private collection. Bottom: typographical compositions for *Zlom* by Karel Teige, Czechoslovakia, 1928. Private collection.

96   Political poster design by Marinetti, Italy, 1930s. Private collection. © DACS 2002.

97/98   Typeface, designer unknown, mid-1900s. Private collection.

99   Cover of *Campo de Grafico*, designer unknown, Italy, 1939.

100   Gothic wood letter, designer unknown, UK, ca 1837.

101   Ilya Zdanevich, title page of *Zohna and Brides*, Russia, ca 1925. Courtesy Misha Anikst.

102   Cover of *Le Mot*, design by Paul Iribe, France, 1915. Courtesy David Batterham.

103   Typeface from the signwriter's manual *Pismo a jeho Konstrukce by* Richard Pípal, Czechoslovakia, 1956. Collection Redstone Press.

104   Symbols from *Typogane*, typefounders' catalogue, Germany, ca 1933. Courtesy Jan Solpera.

105   *Les Catalanes*, a typeface design by Enric Crous-Vidal (never produced) from Caractère Noël, Spain, 1952. Courtesy Fundación Tipográfia Bauer Spain.

106/107   Pages from the Marsh Stencil Machine Co. catalogue, USA, ca 1947. Courtesy collection of Eric Finkel.

108   From the lettering manual by Jan Sembera, Czechoslovakia, 1938. Collection Redstone Press.

109   Josef Síma, cover of *Love Poems* by Otakar Storch-Marien, Czechoslovakia, 1928.

110   Max Burchartz, title page of leaflets for The Motley Square No. 2, Germany, 1924. Courtesy Merrill C. Berman Collection, New York.

111   From promotional folder for *Futura* typeface, 1930s. Courtesy Klingspoor Museum, Germany.

112   Herbert Bayer, Bauhaus leaflet, Germany, 1928. Courtesy Merrill C. Berman Collection, New York. © DACS 2002.

113   Symbols from *Graphic News*, Germany, 1939. Courtesy Verlag Hermann Schmidt, Mainz.

114   Fortunata Depero, collage, Italy, 1928. © DACS 2002.

117   Eye chart instruction cards for patients with hearing difficulties, F. C. Cooper (London mid 20th Century).

117/123   Photographs and eye-test charts from *Eye and Instruments: Nineteenth-century ophthalmological instruments in the Netherlands* by Isolde den Tonkelaar, Harold E. Henkes and Gijsbert K. van Leersum (1996). Courtesy of BV Uitgeverij De Bataafsche Leeuw, Van Soeren and Co. Amsterdam.

118   Snellen optotypes (post-1875).

119   Snellen optotype. Left: For testing astigmatism (ca 1872). Right: Open-sided squares for non-readers (1874).

120   Breslau ophthalmologist Wolffberg's optotypes for children featuring figures and signs (1892).

121   Snellen charts featuring letter types and Snellen's fan for determining the direction of astigmatism (ca 1875).

122   Left: Optotypes in Japanese lettering designed by Ito Gempak who worked with Snellen from 1870 to 1880 (1873). Right: Optotype in Gothic lettering published by H. Peters (Berlin 1873).

123   Left: Snellen chart. Right: Snellen chart with E-figures for non-readers (both post-1875).

124   Hand operated color-mills for testing color recognition. Left: 1860. Right: ca 1875 to 1900.

127   Chinese ideogram with two birds, 18th Century. Courtesy Fang Chen.

128   Cover of *Lettres*, Arts et Métiers Graphiques (Deberny and Peignot, Paris, 1948). Collection Redstone Press.

129/130   *Fregio Mecano*, typeface from a typefounders' catalogue, Italy, ca 1930. Courtesy Pentagram.

131   Cover of *Cobra Norato (Nheengatu du margem esquerda do Amazonas)*, designer unknown, Brazil, 1931. Private collection.

132   Publicity announcement for *Futura* typeface "The type of our time," design by Paul Renner, Germany, 1930, (reproduced in Gebrauchsgraphik, Germany, 1930). Courtesy Gutenberg-Museum, Mainz.

133   Page from *Hoffmann's Schriftatlas*, Julius Hoffmann, Verlag, Germany, 1930. Private collection.

134   Typeface with two styles, France, date unknown. Private collection.

135   Advertisement from Arts et Métiers Graphiques (Deberny and Peignot, Paris, 1930s). Private collection.

136   *Aleksandr Rodchenko, Still Life with Leica*, photograph, Russia, 1930. Courtesy Alexander Lavrentiev, The Rodchenko / Stepanova Archive, Moscow.

137   Aleksandr Rodchenko, front cover of *Conversation with the Finance Inspector about Poetry by Vladimir Mayakovsky*, Russia, 1926. Courtesy, Alexander Lavrentiev, The Rodchenko / Stepanova Archive, Moscow.

138   Top: wrapper for a joke ink-blot made of tin, Germany, ca 1890. Collection Redstone Press. Bottom: from a typefounders' manual, USA, ca 1900. Collection Redstone Press.

139   Edward Wright, drawing for a typeface, UK, 1965. Courtesy Department of Typography and Graphic Communication at The University of Reading.

140   Designs for letterheads reproduced in Typografia XXXVIII, Czechoslovakia, 1930s. Courtesy Museum of Decorative Arts, Prague.

141   Karel Sourek, cover for *Jazz* by E. F. Burian, Czechoslovakia, 1928. Collection Redstone Press.

142   Cover of Arts et Métiers Graphiques (Deberny and Peignot Paris, 1938). Collection Redstone Press.

143   Signwriter's alphabet, from the Rotterdamsche Schilderschool (compiled by A. R. van der Burg, the Netherlands, early-1900s). Courtesy Jan Tholenaar Collection Amsterdam.

144   Hand-drawn typeface, designer unknown, date unknown. Private collection.

145   Advertisement for Wurzburg Brothers (1930s) from *The Encyclopedia of the Packaging Industry*, (Breskin and Charlton Publishing Corporation, New York, 1936). Courtesy Pentagram.

146   From *The Manual of Typefaces* by Richard Pípal, Czechoslovakia, 1956. Collection Redstone Press.

147   Karel Teige, *Untitled*, print with watercolor, Czechoslovakia, 1927. Collection Merrill C. Berman, New York. © The Estate of Karel Teige.

148   Top: cigarette pack designs ("Miss Mend" was the title of a popular series of detective novels), designers unknown, except for top right design by Aleksandr Rodchenko. Courtesy Misha Anikst. Bottom: poster advertising cigarettes. Courtesy Misha Anikst.

149   Russian alphabet probably based on Bodoni, Russia, ca 1890. Private collection.

150   Specimens of embossing by Waterhouse Brothers and Layton Ltd., UK, 1890. Private collection.

151/152/161/162   Design for end-papers by Hiang Kee, UK, 1980. Collection Redstone Press.

153/160 Typeface designs from signwriter's manuals from, *Modèles de Lettres sur vingt tons de fonds differents*, and *Modèles de Lettres pour peintres en bâtiments* (France early-1900s). Courtesy Collinge and Clark.

163 E. Di Vavalcanti, cover design for the journal *Joaquim No. 15*, Brazil, 1947. Private collection.

164 Logotypes from *The Typeface Handbook* by E. Beaufort, Czechoslovakia, ca 1935. Courtesy Museum of Decorative Arts, Prague.

165 Top: typeface from signwriters, manual, Czechoslovakia, 1930s. Collection, Redstone Press. Bottom: Frantisek Zelenka "Three Jazz Reviews," poster, 1930, Czechoslovakia. Courtesy Museum of Decorative Arts, Prague.

166 Menu, designer unknown, from Arts et Métiers Graphiques, (Deberny and Peignot, Paris, 1930s). Collection Redstone Press.

167 Typeface, designer unknown, UK, ca 1890. Collection Redstone Press.

168 Typefaces designed by Paul Carlyle and Guy Oring from *Letters and Lettering* (McGraw-Hill Book Co., USA, 1938). Courtesy Brian Webb Collection.

169 Advertisement for Ever Ready Labels from *The Encyclopedia of the Packaging Industry* (Breskin and Charlton Publishing Corporation, New York, 1936). Courtesy Pentagram.

170/171 Two versions of typeface Patrona Grotesk, designer unknown, date unknown, Czechoslovakia. Courtesy Jan Solpera.

172 Flourishes designed by Enric Crous-Vidal, Spain, 1953. Courtesy Fundación Tipográfica Bauer, Barcelona.

173 Typeface designed by Enric Crous-Vidal, date unknown, Spain. Courtesy Fundación Tipográfica Bauer, Barcelona.

174 Michel Leiris, *Amour*, from *Glossary: Where My Gloss Err*, Paris, 1939. Private collection.

175 Lowercase Slender Roman letters from *Hoffmann's Schriftatlas*, (Julius Hoffmann Verlag Germany, 1930). Private collection.

176 A. M. Cassandre, Bifur, alphabet, France, 1929. Courtesy Klingspoor Museum, Offenbach.

177 Jan Tschichold, poster for opera, *Casanova*, Germany, 1920s, from Gebrauchsgraphik, 1928. Courtesy Gutenberg-Museum, Mainz.

178 Top left: cover of issue of *Campo Grafico* dedicated to Italian Futurism, design by Saladin, Italy, 1942. Private collection. Top right: cover of the issue of *Campo Grafico* dedicated to Italian Futurism, design by Bona, Italy, 1939. Private collection. Bottom left: cover of *Denki Ningyo* (Italian: Fantocci elettrici) designer unknown, Tokyo, 1925. Private collection. Bottom right: announcement of the death of Umberto Boccione in *L'Italia Futurista*, Italy, 1916, (design by Giacomo Balla). Private collection.

179 Gothic Special wood letters designed at the Hamilton Company, USA, ca 1910, from *American Wood Type 1828 to 1900* by Rob Roy Kelly, (Da Capo Press USA, 1977).

180 Typeface design by Morris Fuller Benton, USA, 1935. Private collection.

181 Miroslav Ponc, cover design for Dr. J. Brandenberger 1877 to 1927 (Akrostichon, Prague, 1927). Courtesy City Gallery, Prague.

182 From *Lettres*, Arts et Métiers Graphiques (Deberny and Peignot, Paris, 1948). Collection Redstone Press.

183 Robert Michel, *Collage*, 1927, Germany. Collection Merrill C. Berman, New York.

184 Jan Tschichold, instructional page from *The New Typography*, Germany, 1928. Collection Mel Gooding.

185/186 Pages from *Typographic News*, Germany, 1926. Courtesy Verlag Hermann Schmidt, Mainz.

187 Top: Piet Zwart, from N. C. W. Catalogue, Netherlands, 1928. Collection Merrill C. Berman, New York. © DACS 2002. Bottom: Jan Tschichold, covers for the book *Fototek* nos. 1 and 2, Berlin, 1930. Collection Merrill C. Berman, New York.

188 Promotional brochure, design Kozma, ca 1930. Collection Merrill C. Berman, New York.

189   Page from *Hoffmann's Schriftatlas*, (Julius Hoffmann Verlag Germany, 1930). Private collection.

190   Friedrich Vordemberge-Gildewart designs. Top left/bottom left: covers for the architectural magazine *Forum*, the Netherlands, 1953 to 1951. Top right: Prospectus for Kestner-Gesellschaft, Hanover, 1928. Bottom right: cover for advertising prospectus for the H. Osterwald Printing Works, Hanover, 1927, from *Vordemberge-Gildewart: The Complete Works*, Prestel Verlag. © The Vordemberge-Gildewart Foundation.

191   Stencil alphabet, designer unknown, Russia, ca 1920.

192   I. V. Kliun, watercolor chart from unpublished instructional volume, Moscow, 1942 (ex. Costakis Collection).

195/200   Pages from *Mise En Page: The Theory and Practice of Layout* by A. Tolmer (The Studio Ltd, London, 1932). Courtesy The Department of Typography and Graphic Communication at The University of Reading.

203   Liubov Popova, cover of *Valse* by E Pavlov, Russia, 1922. Private collection.

204   Top left: cover of *Integral*, designer unknown, Romania, 1925. Private collection. Top right: cover of *Blok*, designer unknown, Poland, 1926. Private collection. Bottom left: collage poster design by Mihailo S. Petrov for Zenit exhibition, Yugoslavia, 1924. Private collection. Bottom right: cover design by M. H. Maxy for Contimporanul, Romania, 1924. Private collection.

205   Alphabet design by Cehonin, Russia, 1925. Private collection.

206   Symbols from *Trade Marks and Symbols*, (Graphis, Zurich, 1948).

207   Theatre poster design by Vilmos Huszar, Berlin, 1931. Courtesy Merrill C. Berman Collection, New York.

208   Alphabet design by William Dressler, ca 1950, from *Lettering Art in Modern Use* (Reinhold Publishers, USA, 1952).

209   Photograph of printer-designers, photographer unknown, from *Schriftenproben*, design by Walter Cyliax, (Gebr. Fretz Ab Zurich, 1933). Courtesy Brian Webb Collection.

210   Top: lettering, design by K. C. Aryan from *Calligraphy and Symbols*, India, 1966. Bottom: "Japanese-style" lettering, date unknown. Courtesy Dover Publications.

211   Top: front and back covers of school-book, India, ca 1955. Private collection. Bottom: match-box label, Japan, 1930. Collection Redstone Press

212   A. M. Cassandre, poster for Florent pastilles, published Hachard and Cie, Paris, 1930s. Private collection.

213   A. M. Cassandre, Peignot typeface, Paris, 1937. Private collection.

214   Didot typeface, France, ca 1810. Private collection.

215   From *Le Mot*, design by Paul Iribe, Paris, 1930s. Private collection.